D1175934

Wives, Slaves, and Concubines

Wives, Slaves, and Concubines

A HISTORY OF THE FEMALE UNDERCLASS IN DUTCH ASIA

Eric Jones

NORTHERN ILLINOIS UNIVERSITY PRESS / *DeKalb*

© 2010 by Northern Illinois University Press

Published by the Northern Illinois University Press, DeKalb, Illinois 60115

Manufactured in the United States using postconsumer-recycled, acid-free paper.

All Rights Reserved

Design by Julia Fauci

The photographs used throughout this book are from the John M. Echols Collection on Southeast Asia, Cornell University Library

Library of Congress Cataloging-in-Publication Data

Jones, Eric (Eric Alan)

Wives, slaves, and concubines: a history of the female underclass in Dutch Asia / Eric Jones.

    p.   cm.

Includes bibliographical references and index.

ISBN 978-0-87580-410-1 (clothbound: alk. paper)

1. Women—Indonesia—Social conditions—18th century. 2. Wives—Indonesia—History—18th century. 3. Women slaves—Indonesia—History—18th century.

4. Mistresses—Indonesia—History—18th century. 5. Concubinage—Indonesia—History—18th century. 6. Poor women—Indonesia—History—18th century.

7. Sex role—Indonesia—History—18th century. 8. Marginality, Social—Indonesia—History—18th century. 9. Indonesia—Social conditions—18th century.

10. Netherlands—Colonies—Asia—History—18th century. I. Title.

HQ1752.J66 2010

305.48'96240959809033—dc22

2009048452

To Nyai Ontosoroh

Contents

Acknowledgments

People have commented, upon learning of the focus of my book, that I must have come from a home full of strong women. This is correct, but the women (and men) I grew up with were responsible for much more than a research topic. Two homesteading women from Wyoming—the "Equality State," which was the first in the world to give women the right to vote (1869) and home to more of the nation's firsts for women: first female justice of peace and bailiff (1870), first female jury (1870), first female statewide official (1894), first all-female town government (1920), and first female governor (1924)—left an indelible imprint on their posterity. Granny Cookie's brimming determination (a condition she describes as being "filled with piss and vinegar") and Grandma Vivian's fiery advocacy continue to fill those around them with light and strength. A true cowgirl my mother, Gail, never ceases getting back on that horse, real or metaphorical. It is her unwavering faith in the never-ending abilities and potential of her family that is the engine of our progress.

My father, Wayne, besides being a loving and involved father wisely surveyed the fault-line of historical change that ran through our family farm. His foresight at a moment of great seismic shift and his insistence that I "seek wisdom and learning" (for example by taking high school French and calculus instead of animal husbandry and ag shop) gave me alternatives, including academia. For this I am grateful, though there were nostalgic moments on the long road to tenure where rural poverty seemed a welcome alternative to the academic kind. My older yet close siblings—Jeff, Angela, and Crystal—set personal and professional examples to which I still aspire.

At Hawaii and Berkeley, friends and mentors worked patiently with me as I refined my topic. They include Barbara Andaya, Leonard Andaya, Jeff Belnap, Nelleke van Deusen-Scholl, Jeff Hadler, Carla Hesse, Gene Irschick, Alan Karras, Ninik Lunde, Tom Metcalf, Nancy Peluso, Tony Reid, Johan Snapper, Randy Starn, Jean Taylor, Sylvia Tiwon, Jan de Vries, and Peter Zinoman.

The help, friendship, and "local knowledge" of individuals too numerous to mention made the years spent abroad memorable and enjoyable. In the Netherlands many contributed directly to my research. These include Leonard Blusse, Peter Boomgaard, Peter Christiaans, Wim van den Doel, Femme Gaastra, Frances Gouda, Pieter Koenders, Theo van der Meer, Henk Niemeijer, Remco Raben, Gerritt Knaap, and support personnel at ARA, CBG, KB, UA, UL, KITLV, and TANAP. In Indonesia and Malaysia, those involved in helping and shaping me and my topic include Jim Collins, Darus, Mason Hoadley, Sophie Muzwar, Shamsul, Uri Tadmore, Thee Kian Wie, and others at ANRI, ATMA, IKIP, LIPI, and UKM.

I incurred many debts along the way, human and otherwise, but the financial burden would have been far greater if not for the generous awards of many funding agencies that made this project possible. They include Ehrman Chair Fellowship, Regents Fellowship of the University of California, Humanities Research Grant, UC Grant-in-Aid, Netherlands-America Foundation Nordholt-Leiden History Grant, J. William Fulbright Full Grants to the Netherlands and Malaysia, UC Berkeley Department of History Traveling Fellowship, Foreign Language Area Studies fellowships in Bahasa Indonesian and Afrikaans, Consortium of Teaching Indonesian-Malay (COTIM) Fellowship, Foreign and Domestic Travel Awards from NIU's Center for Southeast Asian Studies, Robbins Fellowship at UC Berkeley's Boalt School of Law, and NIU's Summer Research and Artistry Award.

Friends and colleagues made the journey worthwhile. I thank Kathy Anderson, Taylor Atkins, Maitrii Aung-Thwin, Jim Collins, Chris DeRosa, Sean Farrell, Jeff Hadler, Trude Jacobsen, Andrew Jainchill, Tina Jamaluddin, John Roosa, Dar Rudnyckyj, Priya Satia, Jim Schmidt, Shamsul, Eric Tagliacozzo, Carol Tan, my colleagues at the Center for Southeast Asian

Studies at NIU, and many students for reading over different incarnations of this manuscript and giving freely of their time and insights. Thanks to the students at the San Quentin State Prison College Program who were brave enough to sign up for my "Colonial Literature and History of Indonesia" course and heard so much about my research. I am eternally grateful to Jim Collins at NIU's Center for Southeast Asian Studies, Alex Schwartz at NIU Press, and several anonymous readers for spearheading the book's publication. Jim Schmidt deserves special attention as one of the most gifted academic mentors (and flatpickin' guitarists) around. Having three kids—Taylor, Spencer, and Ethan—has been as crazy as everyone thinks, but their enthusiasm and my fear of not putting food in their mouths has both fed me and made me hungry.

Wives, Slaves, and Concubines

Introduction

The *slavin* or female slave Tjindra van Bali was in bad shape. Her entire face was bruised, she had a small burn on her right cheek, her left ear was torn and her eyelid was mangled, her stomach and back were covered with bruises. A runaway, badly beaten, Tjindra did not make it far before she was picked up by the servants on a neighboring Javanese estate and brought in for medical attention. On 25 April 1775, Tjindra told her attending physician, Batavian city surgeon David Beijlon, how this had happened. Beijlon wrote, "according to her statement, yesterday in the *kampung baru* she was beaten with a slipper, with firewood, and with rattan by her master's wife."[1] Tjindra was the unlucky victim of her mistress, a mestiza Chinese woman named Oetan.[2] Like hundreds of ordinary eighteenth-century Asian women, Tjindra sat down in front of the dutiful scribes of the Batavian Court of Aldermen and talked at length about who she was, where she had been, and what had happened to her.

This study of wives, slaves, and concubines, the female underclass, uses compelling stories from ordinary Asian women such as Tjindra to explore the profound structural changes occurring at the end of the early colonial period, changes that helped birth the modern world order. Based on previously untapped criminal proceedings and testimonies made by women who appeared before the Dutch East India Company's Court of Aldermen, it details the ways in which demographic and economic realities transformed the social and legal landscape of eighteenth-century Batavia (modern-day Jakarta, Indonesia), a bustling hub in the Asian trading network and the colonial capital for the economic superpower of the time, the Republic of the United Netherlands. At this rendezvous, Batavia, men and women met frequently with death but also with each other, so that a diverse and dynamic society evolved. Municipal institutions such as the Court of Aldermen existed to provide order for the women and men living in that entrepot. The investigations and interrogations conducted by the aldermen comprise some of the oldest and it seems the most extensive narrative sources from common men and women in early modern Southeast Asia. The sources paint vivid and captivating pictures of life in Dutch Asia: an abusive mestiza Chinese concubine causes her male slave to run amok; an Ambonese female slave runs away with her goldsmith boyfriend; a female Makassarese slave defrauds Chinese business men using her Arab master's credit.

My investigation develops from three intertwined realities of life in early modern Southeast Asia. We know that Southeast Asian women played an inordinately important role in the functioning of the early modern Asia trade and in the short- and long-term operations of the Dutch East India Company (VOC). Moreover, we have an increasingly clear picture of Southeast Asia as a place where most individuals operated within an intricate web of multiple, fluid, situational and reciprocal social relationships ranging from dependence to bondedness to slavery. In a broader sense, the late eighteenth century represents an important turning point. By then, the relatively open and autonomous Asia trade, which prompted Columbus to set sail at the end of the fifteenth century, began to give way to an age of high imperialism and European economic hegemony. What we do not know is how these realities affected the masses, particularly women. Hence, the book focuses on a couple of simple but momentous questions: What was life like for ordinary women in early modern Dutch Asia? How did the transformations wrought by Dutch colonialism alter their lives?

My argument is that Dutch colonial practice and law created a new set of social and economic divisions in Batavia in order to deal with these Southeast Asian realities. In response, the VOC created a legal division that privileged members of mixed VOC families where Asian women married men who worked for the company. Employment (VOC versus non-VOC) and not race became the path to legal preference. On the one hand, Dutch Asian law privileged Asian Company wives; on the other hand, it disadvantaged the rest of the Asian women under VOC control. In short, colonialism created a new underclass in Asia, one that had a particularly female cast to it. By the latter half of the eighteenth century, an increasingly operational dichotomy of slave and free supplanted an otherwise fluid system of reciprocal bondedness. The inherent divisions of this new system engendered social friction, especially as the emergent early modern economic order demanded new, tractable forms of labor. Dutch domestic law gave power to female elites in Dutch Asia, but it left the majority of women vulnerable to the more privileged on both sides of the legal divide. As reciprocity broke down, slaves fled and violence erupted when their traditional expectations of social mobility collided with the new demands of their masters and the state.

The primary contributions of this book are twofold. First, it reveals the heretofore hidden world of women in the Dutch Asian underclass. Scholars looking for female voices in official VOC archives (sometimes the only extant period records) have mostly been disappointed. A common assumption, especially concerning the state of the archival material before 1900, is that Company collections deal primarily with matters of direct economic profit and therefore contain little of use for narrative social history. Yet, as this book shows, some of the best sources of data on gender and social history have gone untouched. Until this book, no single firsthand biographical narrative has ever been written about a Southeast Asian woman who was non-aristocratic or non-elite. This is the first book to make extensive use of documents in which the voices of non-elite women from early modern Southeast Asia actually speak. Filled with violence, high emotion, and sexual dalliance, the spectacle of the criminal proceedings conveys a human interest value that transcends conventional historical narrative.

Second, this study provides answers to important questions about the workings of mixed ethnic societies, the nexus of crime and gender, and the beginnings of the modern economic world system. It shows that economic pragmatism often took precedence over matters of race in the mixed ethnic societies of the early modern world. It also challenges prevailing assumptions concerning gender and the law by illuminating the ways that varying levels of power, much of it female, can generate violence and criminality. Finally and most important, this book offers a new understanding for the legacies of colonialism. It sheds light on the origins of high imperialism in the nine-teenth century by turning our attention to the social and economic evolution of the late eighteenth. The construction of a colonial underclass in the late eighteenth century served as a necessary precursor for the commodification of human labor that lay at the heart of late Dutch colonialism.

An important backdrop to this enterprise is the scholarly debate concern-ing the uniqueness of the position of women in Southeast Asia and relative lack of sources about them before 1800. Chapter 1 grounds the discussion of the high status and centrality of women (Asian, white, and mestizo) in Southeast Asia and Dutch Asia. It identifies an important problem: while a consensus has emerged around the importance of "high status of women in Southeast Asia," a lack of sources has stymied scholarly attempts to explore this phenomenon in the early modern period. Relying not on the typical official VOC sources, this book draws on the virtually unopened municipal archives of the Batavian Court of Aldermen.

Chapter 2 delves into the demographic and economic constraints that underlay the Dutch presence in Asia and that (both literally and figura-tively) colored colonial society and the experience of Asian women with Roman Dutch law. The ubiquity of interracial mixing between Europeans and Asians, resulting from the lack of European females, pushed colonial officials to choose a legal system that discriminated based on VOC employ-ment and connection rather than race. Malaria drove VOC personnel down—and mixed marriage and remarriage up—thereby checking Euro-peans' aspirations to replicate themselves culturally and genetically in early modern Asia, but it did not check the advance of the Company's economic program. VOC fortunes in the Indies were made not so much from the sweat of the masses (as in the nineteenth and twentieth centuries) but by trading on—and in some cases controlling certain sectors of—the preexist-ing Asian market. The Company had not yet yoked widespread peasant labor and therefore did not need to reduce the legal standing of indigenous peoples to that of draft animals. If demographics coaxed Company men into the arms of Asian brides, economics allowed the VOC to see Asians as equals under the law or not to see them at all.

Chapter 3 examines, for the first time, how the VOC found its recipe for success in eschewing ideology in the regulation of marriage, family, and household economics and in the design of its legal architecture. In the existing literature, the success of the Dutch East India Company is often attributed to its very innovative and deliberate approach to the Asian trade network: enormous capital investments in Asia, long-term business planning, monopolizing the supply chain, and the like. While this is true, and these are important components to VOC's preeminence, another understated yet overarching ideal is vital in explaining the operations and behaviors of the Company. Perhaps the most central organizing principle to the Dutch East India Company was the principle without principles—pragmatism. The same spirit animated the VOC approach to Company wives, families, and colonial law itself. In an examination of the Company's approach to mixed marriage and a dual court system, we find that the VOC constructed a local legal framework in its Southeast Asian territories around two important considerations: first, the desire to protect and promote VOC employees and their mostly Asian dependents; and second, to discriminate not by race but by whether someone was Company or non-Company, thus privileging VOC families and excluding their European rivals, namely, the British. The same pragmatic spirit animating the VOC's approach to colonial law also conditioned the Company's response to the demographic and economic forces defining its jurisprudence.

In Chapter 4, I argue that female slaves in VOC-controlled Southeast Asia did not fare well under a legal code that erected a firm partition between free and slave status. This codification imposed a rigid dichotomy for what had previously been fluid, abstract conceptions of social hierarchy and, in effect, silted up the flow of underclass mobility. At the same time, conventional relationships between master and slave shifted in the context of a changing economic climate. Chapter 4 closely narrates the lives of eighteenth-century female slaves who, left with fewer and fewer options within this new order, resorted to running away. Of particular interest to the outside reader is a comparative discussion of slavery in Asia versus that in the New World—and a challenge to prevalent assumptions concerning the larger history of slavery, that is, that the Atlantic world is the anomaly and the Indian Ocean world is the norm for most of human history.

The cases investigated in Chapter 5 focus on women who abused their inferiors. It delivers dramatic evidence of how differently the demographic constraints and financial priorities of the Dutch East India Company that brought some Asian women into its "family" (as shown in Chapter

3) played out for the rest of the Asian women in the colonies under its legal authority. These stories demonstrate an important tension in colonial society and highlight a critical moment in the modern world economic system. Masters and mistresses no longer felt vertically bonded with their subjects in terms of reciprocal relationships of dependency. Instead, their interests in their underlings became primarily economic and their behavior followed suit. We see how the occasional woman from the Asian underclass resorted to excessive violence when dealing with the men and women who were her social inferiors and ended up telling her story to the Court of Aldermen. Together the cases share important traits, clues about the construction of female violence in Batavia.

The Conclusion of this study takes the themes developed throughout the preceding chapters and projects them forward into the nineteenth and twentieth centuries. I firmly establish the eighteenth century as a pivotal moment between a previous early modern condition of relative Southeast Asian autonomy and the more well-known oppression of the pervasive plantation economy that would come to typify the high imperialism of the late modern era. I advocate that an understanding of the structural and social transformations that occurred before 1800 is vital to comprehending the culmination of those late colonial labor and economic structures, and local resistance to it. The Conclusion highlights a critical waning moment in the shift away from something like autonomous, if not independent, participation in the global economic system by European and Asian actors.

The Court of Aldermen records straddle that indefinite historical fulcrum, one side of which we can imagine as another world that might have been, while the other side we must recognize as a watershed that we in the present have yet to move beyond. As the relationship between Europe and Southeast Asia became more lopsided and sour, we smell the demise of a colonial order with a law code that treated Europeans and Asians alike, a society that embraced racial mixing, an economy that was not yet fueled by widespread agrarian labor under colonial control. We watch the approach of the modern imperial order where plural (in the negative sense) and divided societies walk a tense line, imperial governments live in fear of racial contamination, and Southeast Asian poverty is institutionalized.

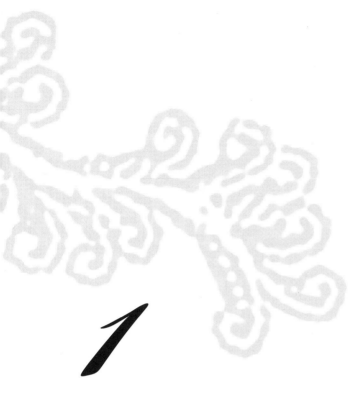

Gender, Bondage, and the Law in Early Dutch Asia

Women in Dutch Asia

This study focuses on the women of Dutch Asia in the early modern era, in particular those *slavinnen*, concubines, and women of the underclass who were brought to the courthouse to testify.[1] However, not all women in the VOC-controlled enclaves identified (or were identified) with that large cohort. Some Asian and Eurasian women married employees of the Dutch East India Company and thereby acquired European legal status. The few studies that focus directly on this VOC female population have drawn attention to the surprising amount of power and influence these Company wives exerted in the colonies. They seemed to have possessed something that we could call "high status." Apparently, they were not alone.

Much of the literature on women in non-European Southeast Asia makes similar claims for their respective female populations: that they had a relatively high status. Although the women of the underclass and those with European status even when ethnically identical led very different lives, important connections link the two groups. The legal system that arose for the sake of the Company wives in criminal affairs also prevailed upon Batavia's female underclass. These disparate, yet converging, literatures about women in Dutch Asia and Southeast Asia share essential assumptions but also suggest many scholarly avenues yet to be explored. Although some literatures have pointed to the centrality of Asian women in Indies society and others have chosen the high status of Southeast Asian women as a key topic of debate, there has been a general consensus that the archives are disappointing as a source for the history of women in early modern Southeast Asia.

The first scholarly foray into the subject appeared in F. C. de Haan's urban history of the Dutch colonial capital, *Oud Batavia*, published in 1922. Although de Haan predates the high status theories, his basic portrayal of women in Dutch Asia is the baseline for all subsequent studies. Initially, the colonial government commissioned *Oud Batavia* as a not-too-rigorous tricentennial history of Batavia in the Company period for lay and learned readers alike. World War I intervened, delaying the publication but also allowing Batavian state archivist de Haan the freedom to write his classic history in an expanded form. The text is dense and lacks a tight organization, including neither footnotes nor citations, but it does contain many of the insights and observations about the women of Dutch Asia that are still with us (only partly because they were correct). Women are not treated in a separate chapter (nor would this be common in history books for another sixty years), but they do appear as he moves across the civic landscape. De Haan's method for describing the population is "climbing from lower to higher, that is, from the slave to the free native inhabitants, from these to the foreign Orientals, the native Christians and the mestizos, eventually ending up with the European element."[2] Because of his style, also, it can be difficult to get a sense of the totality of women's experience.

Later quantitative evidence—such as Remco Raben's dissertation, *Batavia and Colombo: The Ethnic and Spatial Order of Two Colonial Cities, 1600–1800*—substantiates de Haan's model of slave immigration. In the first half of the seventeenth century, Batavia's slaves came primarily from the Indian subcontinent, later they originated within the archipelago (mostly Eastern Indonesia). De Haan's next observation is more difficult to prove: he provides a charming Horatio Alger–like picture of happy, well-treated, blue-collar, industrious slaves-as-entrepreneurs working their way out of slavery through their bakeries and cobblers' benches. Idyllic it may not have been, but it is true that these were not plantation slaves. "Batavia was no Virginia," he said, acknowledging that a different notion of free versus slave operated in Southeast Asia and Batavia than elsewhere. In his section on slaves, de Haan also manages to capture and perpetuate a recurring image of native women as agents who are corrosive to Europeanness in the colonies. According to de Haan the biggest problem with the "native nursemaid" was the kind of behavior she reinforced in the children in her care. The power that European children possessed over their slaves corrupted absolutely: "The keeping of slaves was as demoralizing for the master. The sense of power is always pernicious to [those of] weak and common character. Naturally the children suffered by being among slaves, to whom they could do whatever they pleased and who answered to their angry whims in wheedling and soft tones."[3] In order to combat this behavior, "the Dutch sent their sons to be brought up in Europe to remove them from this environment." Girls in this environment did not have the same luxury as their brothers; instead "the daughters remained in Batavia and grew up to be the most impossible housewives and mothers." This last image—of the impossible "untamable" female product of the Indies—is his most enduring image of Company women and has persisted in historians' accounts.[4]

De Haan's portrayal of mestizo and European women in Dutch Asia uses the absence of the latter to explain the presence of the interracial marriage. The Dutch men "didn't want to marry the natives," but in the absence of Dutch women, he stated, they took concubines. Then de Haan smartly shifts the focus off the marriage versus concubinage dichotomy. "The question," he asserts, "is less of their [mestizo offspring's] lawful birth than of their number and societal position," a position that was high status. According to de Haan, the VOC had complete control over the racial and interracial fate of Batavia but not with the Company's ineffective edits and prohibitions. If the Company had encouraged and allowed the passage of more Dutch women and paid the European burghers a decent wage, then a Dutch population would have predominated instead of the mestizo society that prevailed well into the nineteenth century. De Haan discusses this sensitive topic in quite neutral terms: he simply contrasts VOC policy with late colonial policy, demonstrating that the Dutch under Company rule followed Portuguese practice.[5]

It was another half century before the next important treatment of the women of Dutch Asia appeared. Jean Gelman Taylor's *The Social World of Batavia: European and Eurasian in Dutch Asia* is the only work of its kind, a book-length study of the early modern women of Dutch Asia. Greatly influenced by de Haan, Taylor closely follows many of the arguments set out in *Oud Batavia*. Her point of departure is her focus on Batavia's female elite and the Indies clan system that evolved in this unique historical setting. Taylor's thesis is straightforward. Structural constraints such as the great time and distance between colony and metropole and the high mortality rates for Europeans afforded the colonies a great deal of autonomy and kept the relative numbers of Europeans, especially women, low. VOC policy would not allow men to promote their own kin so they instead began promoting their brothers-in-law and sons-in-law. Marriage and remarriage gave many women access to more position and privilege. A VOC Indies clan system developed in which money and power followed key women and their daughters. In turn, enterprising men began seeking out those women with useful connections.

Most of Taylor's book is devoted to exploring the "social world" of Batavia and how Asian forms and customs inundated European culture and society. Taylor uses Batavian displays of pomp and circumstance as a lodestone to locate the cultural center of gravity in Dutch Asia. Grand Sunday processions of the Batavian women to church shocked Dutch newcomers to Batavia in the VOC period. These women would parade through the streets in elaborate and expensive gowns, followed by large retinues of slaves and retainers. Particularly troubling to some observers were the Asian status symbols that accompanied the women: betel boxes, parasols, and so on. One specific "Asian" model for women that Taylor points out in Batavia was the cloistering of the elite. Far from evidence of mobility and independence, she draws attention to "the fact that church attendance was one of the few outings elite women took." The reclusion of elite women evolved "not from imitation of the bourgeoisie in the Netherlands, but from increased familiarity with Asian civilizations and with the habits of the Portuguese overseas."[6] Taylor uses a wide range of mostly secondary sources and provides fresh glimpses into the important role of Asian women in the Dutch enclaves of Asia. While undoubtedly the most important monograph on the subject, Taylor's, like others, relies heavily on European travelers' accounts for insights into the women of Dutch Asia. In any event, her inspiring work belongs in the canon of Southeast Asian histories and can be considered the wellspring of much subsequent work on gender and empire, including this one.

In the last twenty years several scholars have also begun researching the female population of the enclaves of Dutch Asia. Some of the most important work has been done by those working on urban history in the VOC era. Important contributions such as Leonard Blussé's *Strange Company,* Remco Raben's *Batavia and Colombo,* and Henk Niemeijer's *Calvinisme en koloniale stadscultuur Batavia* have added a richness of detail and important empirical evidence to our understanding of the colonial capital in the VOC period. Blussé, Raben, Niemeijer, Susan Abeyasekere, and others have firmly established the essentially Asian character of Batavia— demonstrated in terms of mixed marriages, urban design, and religious practice.[7] In addition, Blussé combed colonial and municipal archives to paint a narrative portrait of a feisty and powerful VOC bride, Cornelia Nijenrode. Finally, a recent volume edited by Barbara Watson Andaya and entitled *Other Pasts: Women, Gender, and History in Early Modern Southeast Asia,* brought together scholars such as Gerritt Knaap, Dhiravat na Pomberja, and again Henk Niemeijer, focusing on women in various VOC stations.[8] Niemeijer's contribution, in particular, was significant in that it was one of the first article-length treatments of non-elite women in early modern Southeast Asia, noting that "while the apex of status and authority was undoubtedly the European-dominated urban middle class . . . other segments of society were clearly visible." Mining the notarial archives in Jakarta, Niemeijer demonstrated that it was possible to write the history of Batavian women outside Taylor's jet set. He persuasively argued that despite colonial categories in the early modern period, factors such as status and simple geographic proximity in Batavia were potentially more important to one's identity than the constructs of race and ethnicity.[9]

In the late nineteenth and twentieth centuries, Asian and mestizo women began losing their place at the center of the colonial social world to the influx of European women arriving on fast steamships through the much shorter Suez route to Asia. A growing body of literature addresses the experience of women and gender in this late colonial period. Often these works focus not only on gender but also on the female "colonizers"—as opposed to the preoccupation of early modern studies with elite Asian women in the colonies (largely in response to the archives).[10] Lured by the temporal proximity of the postcolonial to the colonial, a growing number of articles and edited volumes have appeared, reading the ethnographies of the present into the colonial past.[11]

Of this group, the most influential and widely read of the late colonial or postcolonial scholars on gender and the Dutch East Indies is Ann Stoler. As an anthropologist, Stoler brings valuable interdisciplinary concerns and methods to bear on the study of colonial history, which set her work apart from the work of many other scholars who address the subject. Her insights compel historians to think more carefully about questions of gender and identity in the colonial context. In addition, Stoler's work has served as an entry point for many nonspecialists to Southeast Asia and has redirected historical attention to the importance of the Dutch in an impacted field of colonial studies that seems to dwell exclusively on the British empire. Her writings to date advance at least two central claims: first that colonialism was more of a cultural endeavor than an economic endeavor; and second that not enough attention has been directed toward the colonizer. The review of colonial scholarship in her book points to the economic preoccupations of earlier studies such as James Scott's *Moral Economy of the Peasant* and Clifford Geertz's *Agricultural Involution*.[12] According to Stoler, by focusing on the power of the "structural constraints of colonial capitalism" to shape, destroy, and preserve indigenous communities, scholars have paid too little attention to the colonizer and too much attention to material constraints. Her position is that colonialism was primarily a cultural enterprise, as opposed to an economic venture, adding that few students of empire would claim otherwise.[13]

Stoler rightly criticized "the determinism that some of those [economic] approaches applied," but she failed to acknowledge the profound impact of certain structural factors on cultural forms.[14] Insights into the nature of power and hegemony remind us that force or forces—whether martial, cultural, economic, even structural or environmental—rarely work in simple top-down fashion. Once one strips away the iron law of the historical dialectic, the teleological excesses of Marxism, and the arrogant predictability of environmental determinism, however, materialism remains a useful tool for understanding the colonial experience. Somewhere on the continuum between destiny and agency, geography and demographics laid down the limits of the possible in the Indies. Fernand Braudel believed that "every great center of population has worked out a set of elementary answers—and has an unfortunate tendency to stick to them out of that force of inertia which is one of the greatest artisans of history."[15] The two-year roundtrip from the Netherlands to Java and the 50 percent mortality rate of newcomers to Batavia established certain fundamental rules for early modern colonial existence that no amount of sentiment could change, namely, that the numeric presence of European men would be ephemeral and that of European women nonexistent. Simple structural realities set the boundaries for cultural concerns, racial prejudices, and fear of miscegenation. These demographic facts of life marked out the field of play in which colonial culture then exercised its agency.

Stoler's approach is more nuanced than the simple trumpeting of culture and the denial of structural forces. She makes the important distinction between prescription and practice, noting that colonial aims toward white endogamy were at times little more than wishes, expressed in contrast to the mestizo reality. She questions categories, especially colonial categories, in the study of empire. In her view colonial studies, especially those with an economic focus, often collapse the colonial state, industrial capital, and the European community into an undifferentiated monolith. In her examination of sex and sex ratios among the fractured European community of late nineteenth- and early twentieth-century Deli, Stoler rightly notes that modern scholarship employs great care to avoid Orientalizing distinct non-European communities but that it is seldom so careful when studying the European colonizers. Those striving to go "beyond Orientalism" are often checked by their own clumsy Occidentalization of all things European. In *Carnal Knowledge and Imperial Power*, Stoler advises scholars to focus their ethnographic attention on the European colonizers and not just on the colonized. She welcomes the impulse in new colonial history "to identify the active agency of colonized populations as they engaged and resisted colonial impositions and transformed the terms of that encounter" but laments the fact that "anthropology's ethnographic subject" still remained non-Europeans.[16] Her critique, while useful, is better aimed at those contemporary anthropologists who favor the "colonized" over the "colonizer" as their object of study. In terms of historical research, the opposite seems to be the case. Most historians working on the period still focus on European expansion rather than on domestic Asian history, even though the case for the latter was made passionately in the 1930s by Jacob van Leur—and persuasively somewhat later by John Smail:

> All I have been trying to do for the moment is to awaken the thought that there is an authentic Indonesian body beneath the clothes we call the Netherlands Indies, that this body has its own history, autonomous in the fundamental sense. I am arguing that we are dealing with a society that is coherent and alive and not merely a rubble used by the Dutch for a new building, a society which, by being alive, generates its own history—which like any other history must be seen first of all from the inside—and does not merely receive it.[17]

WOMEN IN EARLY MODERN SOUTHEAST ASIA

The literature on women in Southeast Asia is problematic for understanding the women of Dutch Asia in particular. Following J. C. van Leur's call for a non-Europe-centered autonomous history of Southeast Asia, the last few generations of historians of the early modern era have rightly focused on non-European elements of Southeast Asia. More recently, Southeast Asian women have received a fair amount of attention, resulting in new and important insights into the "status of Southeast Asian women," insights that may or may not apply to the women of Dutch Asia in the early modern era.

Especially when compared with their East Asian counterparts, women in Southeast Asia seem to have enjoyed a relatively high degree of autonomy. Chinese, Arab, and European visitors to the region seldom failed to mention the important, sometimes leading, role played by women in commercial, political, and sexual spheres. Evidence for this phenomenon is found in indigenous and traveler accounts, law codes, and various local political and social practices, all of which present a compelling case for the high status of Southeast Asian women.

Pulling together an array of primary and secondary sources, Anthony Reid's *Southeast Asia in the Age of Commerce* has been the most influential and widely read contribution to the "high status" school of thought. Reid outlines specifically how divorce, commercial, and political practices all contributed to this unique situation in which "Southeast Asian women were playing an unusually influential role by comparison with later periods or with other parts of the world."[18] Several factors made divorce in early modern Southeast Asia both easy and frequent. Bilateral kinship, as opposed to primogeniture, gave women equal access to family wealth and status by allowing property to pass through male and female lines, much as in the Netherlands. The bride price, paid by the groom's family before marriage, became the property of the bride upon divorce, along with half of the divorced couple's combined estate. This lessened the financial leverage a husband might have over his wife, which might otherwise compel her to remain in an unhappy marriage. In addition, a husband generally went to live with his wife's family where she was surrounded by a network of kin support. This acted as a check upon the husband's behavior and made divorce a viable option for women. Furthering the freedom and economic independence enjoyed by women was the general absence of social stigma attached to widows and divorcees. Society tended not to be preoccupied with virginity or sexual purity as a prerequisite to marriage, which made remarriage or living single easy alternatives to a failed marriage.

Sailors and traders who came to Southeast Asia on the trade winds formed liaisons and "temporary" marriages with local women in Southeast Asia. These were no mere "comfort women," they were doorways to local markets. Barbara N. Ramusack has observed that "the men [foreign traders] provided gifts and contacts to outside trading networks, and the women reciprocated with links to local economies, knowledge of indigenous conditions, family support groups, and sexual relations."[19] In the early modern Netherlands, women were allowed into the commercial sphere; in Southeast Asia, women were at its very center. Likewise, Thomas Stamford Raffles, British interregnum governor general of Java between 1811 and 1815, also saw the pivotal place of women in the economy: "It is usual for the husband to entrust his pecuniary affairs entirely to his wife. The women alone attend the markets, and conduct all the business of buying and selling. It is proverbial to say the Javanese men are fools in money concerns."[20] Two centuries of Dutch presence failed to change this Southeast Asian gender role. The Dutch adopted the "women in the marketplace" model and used it throughout the Company period of the seventeenth and eighteenth centuries.

It is no coincidence that the age of commerce also was the age of women in important political positions in Southeast Asia. In order to protect their investments, merchants and the commercially minded aristocracy and oligarchy became increasingly influential in the political sphere and increasingly chose women over men for their monarchs. "In choosing to put women on the throne the *orangkaya* [literally, the "rich people"] were opting not only for mild rule but for businesslike rule. As in other fields, men were expected to defend a high sense of status and honour on the battlefield but to be profligate with their wealth. It was women's business to understand market forces, to drive hard bargains, and to conserve their capital."[21]

Because status was more prominent than gender, "female rule was one of the few devices available to a commercially oriented aristocracy to limit the despotic powers of kings and make the state safe for international commerce." Jacob van Neck, one of the earliest Dutch merchants in the Indies, noted the difference in the late sixteenth century: "[the queen of Patani] has reigned very peaceably with her councilors . . . so that all the subjects consider her government better than that of the dead king. For all necessities are very cheap here now, whereas in the king's time (so they say) they were dearer by half, because of the great exactions which then occurred."[22] In a world where the political engine was oiled by the smooth circulation of capital and gauged according to supply and demand, the interests of the moneyed were in the perpetuation of a fiscally pragmatic state.

Barbara Watson Andaya is less sure about the "high status" of Southeast Asian women. In "The Changing Religious Role of Women in Pre-modern Southeast Asia," Andaya problematizes the position of women in Southeast Asia by shifting the grounds for comparison and by pointing to the different beliefs and social practices that cast doubt on their high status. Premodern and early modern women in Southeast Asia may have appeared dominant and free, says Andaya, because scholars have measured their status "using an Indian or Chinese yardstick." Her point is that, in the land of the blind, the one-eyed man or woman may fare well, but next to the women of fourteenth century Mali, for example, where Ibn Battuta observed that women "'were treated with more respect than men' and that descent was calculated through the female line," Southeast Asian women might not seem so exceptional.[23] This is an interesting argument, but Andaya's own comparative evidence is weak. Granted, her short article is a "preliminary foray into an area as yet relatively unexplored," but more extensive comparative histories on women concede (sometimes in spite of their best efforts) that there is something unusual about the status of women in Southeast Asia.[24]

Andaya's more convincing argument about the ambiguity of Southeast Asian women's status is waged in the Southeast Asian context itself. There are many examples of Southeast Asian belief in the supernatural, magical powers of women to create, heal, and intercede with the spirit world that would seem to add weight to their exceptional position. This can be deceiving, according to Andaya, for the "non-maleness" of the female was venerated and "considered vital for the proper functioning of the world, but only if the correct balance were maintained." Especially in the religious sphere, it was not women per se who were revered but those men who "embodied both male and female" and unlike women did not menstruate. Andaya partially concedes that "their role in food production and trade, the looseness of pre-modern state structures, the entrenched views of male-female dualities in kinship relations" helped women to maintain a comparatively "high status," but their true subordination came through world religions. Indeed, Andaya ultimately staked her claim of Southeast Asian "women's lesser position" on world religions and the ritual non-participation of women in them. Andaya gives examples of how Hindu statuary emphasized the *linga* over the *yoni*, the institutionalization of Theravada Buddhism restricted the role of spirit mediums (many of whom were women) in mainland Southeast Asia, Meccan fatwas forbade women from ruling in Aceh, later Confucianism downplayed the role of women in popular mythology in Vietnam, and Christian chastity circumscribed the sexual freedoms of women in the Philippines. "To these [restrictions]," according to Andaya, "were added political and legal systems that affirmed women's lesser position." These institutional aspects of world religions may have done discursive violence to women's status (and real violence to those women close to the institution), but one is left to wonder as to the consequences of world religions when their effects on the Southeast Asian population at large have been shown to be marginal at best. Could this "thin and flaking glaze" really have constricted Southeast Asian women?[25]

Andaya is also editor of the most significant collection to date of histories of women in Southeast Asia, *Other Pasts: Women, Gender and History in Early Modern Southeast Asia,* and sole author of the most important monograph on the topic, *The Flaming Womb: Repositioning Women in Early Modern Southeast Asia.* Together the works mark a tipping point in the inclusion of gender as part of the writing of Southeast Asian history. Andaya charts previous historical trends and developments, helping to triangulate gender and "herstory" within the literature. She underscores several important factors that have hindered historical work on women in Southeast Asia: the predominance of political history and the paucity of historical sources.

As Andaya points out, some of the earliest historical work that envisioned Southeast Asia as a region (instead of the pre–World War II paradigm, which imagined that corner of the world in its constituent colonial parts) took note of the peculiarly high status of women throughout Southeast Asia. This preliminary observation, however, did not lead to further investigation. Instead, advocates of the high status paradigm frequently used it as a trope to justify the coherence of Southeast Asia as a single unit of study. Connected to postwar geopolitical pressures to view the region as a strategic block, the preeminence of a particular style of political history has been the most stifling (in terms of the historiography) to the study of women and gender in Southeast Asia. Citing Ruth McVey, Andaya explains the "regnant paradigm" of historical research on Southeast Asia. Most roads of postwar historical inquiry led straight to the then political concerns of the moment: the Cold War, nationalism, and economic development.[26] Excluding other historical avenues of departure, solutions to the present were sought by interrogating the past. In Andaya's view, moreover, political histories continue to dominate the field of Southeast Asian history.

Even much of the historical work without this bias toward public policy looked ahead toward national independence, the terminus for the colonial epoch. Researchers set to work, knowing their answers in advance, covering the appropriate historical moments that would lead them to those ends, showing why peasants revolt and where revolutionary movements started, and explaining regional poverty. The special bias in Southeast Asian history toward the narrative of high political history left women largely out of the story. According to Andaya, "good history" was defined as national history. Themes focusing on political figures, and international and military affairs (all spheres thoroughly dominated by men) proved "highly resistant" to the incorporation of women's perspectives.[27] As Andaya has also pointed out, that line of inquiry is not only highly resistant to the inclusion of historical actors outside the traditional nationalist pantheon. Attempts to add a female gloss to what has largely been a male tale can be equally unsatisfying. For historians of the twentieth century, understanding the rise of new Southeast Asian nations and their resistance to old colonial states is an undeniably important endeavor. Historians of early modern Southeast Asia, however, have the luxury of operating in a period where there is a range of possibilities outside the postcolonial nation state for the peoples and places in the region.

In her introduction, Barbara Andaya identified another, more enduring hurdle to writing on women and gender in Southeast Asian history: a lack of sources. The further back in time, the more acute the problem becomes. Andaya noticed a significant drop in available records from before 1900: "for those working on Southeast Asia who are anxious to push back the terrain of inquiry beyond the twentieth century, there remains the fundamental problem of data." Developments and successes in the writing of European history have encouraged historians of Southeast Asia to focus on women and gender, but unfortunately, as Andaya lamented, "a whole range of sources like village registers, school records, memoirs, letters" that made the "explosion of social history" for Europe and America possible "are largely unavailable in Southeast Asia, even in recent times."[28] She concluded by mentioning that one of her reasons for organizing a volume on women in early modern Southeast Asia was "because I was disturbed that historians of the region had made so few contributions to this important field. The absence of relevant research was becoming especially marked as social scientists themselves looked to supply a historical basis for the contemporary situation."[29] In another work, she states, "Southeast Asian historians are painfully aware . . . that surviving documents represent only a fraction of what was once available. In a tropical climate, bark, palm leaf, bamboo, and paper all have an ephemeral life, and over the centuries untold material, both local and foreign, has been lost through natural catastrophe, warfare, or simple carelessness."[30]

Andaya's sentiments echo those of others who have stared into what seemed at the time an archival abyss. In their earlier collection of essays on Indonesian women, editors Elsbeth Locher-Scholten and Anke Niehof cite increased interest in topics concerning women and gender, but they also mention the "main problem" of sources. They add that the sources were "severely limited in scope, especially when it comes to the consideration of the role of women in Indonesian society." Locher-Scholten and Niehof claim that "colonial civil servants evinced scant [academic] interest in Indonesian women," and that "up to about the 1920s, the colonial archives are a disappointing source for those interested in female activities."[31] In the same volume, Peter Carey and Vincent Houben conclude, "The history of women in pre-twentieth-century Java has still to be written. One of the most important problems confronting any scholar wishing to embark on this important subject lies in the nature of the sources. The vast mass of Dutch colonial records, on the whole, pay scant attention to women."[32]

In summary, the literature on women in Southeast Asian history paints an overall picture of relative archival silence. Scholars looking for female voices in official VOC archives (sometimes the only extant period records) have been disappointed. A common assumption, especially concerning the state of the archival material before 1900, is that Company collections deal primarily with matters of direct economic profit and therefore contain little of use for narrative social history. In reality, however, some of best sources of data on gender and social history have gone untouched.

Founded in 1602, the Verenigde Oost-Indische Compagnie (VOC) was a Dutch trading company established by traders and burghers from port towns such as Amsterdam, Rotterdam, and Middelburg. The VOC developed numerous trading activities with countries in and around Monsoon Asia: from Mocha to Java, from Capetown to Canton, from Colombo to Deshima. These endeavors resulted not only in warehouses packed with spices, textiles, porcelain, and silk but also in shiploads of documents. Locally stationed Company officials produced most of the VOC paperwork. Other documentation came from the peoples with whom they interacted: kings and noblemen, traders and middlemen, shippers and *shahbandars* (harbormasters).

The enormous information network that the VOC built up for its business operations is impressive indeed. Data on political, economic, cultural, religious, and social circumstances on sites spread over a huge area circulated among hundreds of VOC offices and establishments and the administrative center in Batavia (modern-day Jakarta). Four shelf-kilometers (25 million pages) of VOC records survive in archives located on three continents. They comprise the vast holdings of VOC archives in Jakarta itself (1,800 shelf-meters), Colombo (310 shelf-meters), Chennai (64 shelf-meters), Cape Town (325 shelf-meters), and The Hague (1,330 shelf-meters).[33]

As deposits of the world's first multinational corporation, the Overgekomen Brieven en Papieren (OBP)—Received Letters and Papers, that is, letters and papers sent from Asia to the Company board of directors in the Netherlands (representing much of the VOC archive now residing in The Hague)—could also be classified as "highly resistant" to the inclusion of women in the overall historical narrative. These reports are rich and detailed but were produced as instruments for corporate analysis. As such, they deal with female slaves, for example, only in terms of the total number bought and sold at auction or living in a quarter of a city in any given year. Some historians have expressed frustration because few female voices appear in these largely financial and political records. The woefully underexplored National Archives of Indonesia contain many of the original Company reports upon which the OBP are based, but this fact does not change their fundamental quantitative focus. Those searching only among the official Company records miss some of the best sources for social history.

The VOC was at heart a corporation with financial interests, but its survival necessitated the creation of supporting civic and municipal institutions in Company-controlled enclaves. Notaries, aldermen, poor-relief agencies, orphanages, land trustees, churches, synods, and other institutions, all performed vital community services on the ground but remained to varying degrees administratively separate from the VOC, as did their archives. These local organizations made and recorded frequent interventions into the lives of ordinary people on the street, most of whom came from the Asian underclass.[34] In many instances, these unconventional colonial sources are the only records available for understanding firsthand the experience of the common Southeast Asian man or woman.

Because of the VOC presence (and accompanying institutions) throughout

Asia and Africa, its colonial sources are among the most important collection of documents for world history in the early modern period, and for women's history in particular. The exceedingly rare pre-nineteenth-century Asian sources mentioning women tend to be of the "travel" variety (in most cases, Chinese). In courtly edicts or epic poems, elite women (if any) are only of passing mention, and still we hear nothing from women on the ground. The further we move back into history, the more indispensable the Dutch colonial archives become. Indonesia's great historian, Sartono Kartodirdjo, proclaimed this fact in a book chapter entitled "The Decolonization of Indonesian Historiography." He wrote that decolonization did "not imply a break away from Dutch sources," and he recognized their value to such an extent that he declared the "ability to read Dutch is a *conditio sine qua non* for Indonesian historians."[35]

Turning from the usefulness of the "non-Company" colonial archive for social history in general, the records of the Court of Aldermen are a particularly productive—yet challenging—source for writing about the Asian multitude. A subsequent chapter of my book covers the history of the aldermen and their legal procedures in detail but, in short, the *Schepenbank* (Court of Aldermen) was a Dutch judicial institution imported to its colonies. In areas such as Batavia, where the VOC exercised direct control over the land and its non-VOC inhabitants, the colonial government set up a Roman Dutch legal apparatus in order to establish some sense of municipal order. The law was exacting and demanded mountains of paperwork (indictments, depositions, interrogations, confessions, medical reports, and so on) as the Batavian Court of Aldermen worked through the numerous cases it heard each year (many of them dealing with women). These accounts provide the most substantial and wide-ranging source on early modern Southeast Asian women, and until now they have been overlooked.[36]

HISTORY AND CRIME IN THE ARCHIVES

History from criminal records is an exercise in schadenfreude: the more interrogations conducted and the more witnesses hauled in for questioning, the more material for the historian. Documents from the darkest moments in a person's life detail hidden corners of the past. Does one hope for the successful flight of a female slave such as Tjindra van

Bali (see Chapter 4), running from a sadistic mistress? If so, Tjindra might have lived free, but she would have remained dead to history. Alternatively, does one wish for the continued success of the aldermen in enforcing laws—laws that seem unjust to modern sensibilities—in return for their detailed records? A successful slavin escape translates into archival failure. Had there been no capture, there would have been no interrogation, no trial, no witnesses, and no historical record of her life. Her arrest and investigation deliver unparalleled insights (even Tjindra's own) into her world and society at large. Ironically, the aldermen's prosecutory zeal to aggressively regulate and contain individuals whose behavior threatened a juridical and social order has collected, preserved, and historically immortalized the very thing it sought to eliminate.

As a historian, I am not interested in retrying the case, nor am I interested in the same kinds of truths that interested the aldermen and the defendants. More than two centuries later, the "true" guilt or innocence of a given defendant is no longer the important question. Instead, the cases reveal larger social truths. In their edited volume of Italian historical research on crime, Edward Muir and Guido Ruggiero explain the significance of using criminal records to "read" a society: "A crime is a moment when a culture fails in its own terms, a moment when microsystems challenge macrosystems of power and values." From the actions taken by the courts to the strategies employed by the defendants, the criminal event forces the articulation and execution of ideologies that otherwise might never surface, in addition to resurrecting "the otherwise hidden life of the street, gaming hall, counterfeiter's workshop, priest's bedroom, and prison cell."[37]

Still, though criminal records hold great potential as historical source material, they are far from transparent. Just as the Batavian legal system subjected Asian women and men to relentless questioning and searing skepticism, so too must the criminal archive itself undergo rigorous interrogation and be met with sustained caution from the historian. What does one do with a confession extracted under torture, a statement made under duress, or a self-serving testimony? How mediated is a story from a slavin's subjective memory, told in Malay to Asian and European scribes? Can the subaltern speak frankly without fear of retribution? Is a separate autonomous history possible, given the nature of these sources? What are the alternatives when faced with these problematic but extraordinarily rich historical documents?[38]

The leading lights of microhistory, Carlo Ginzburg, Natalie Zemon Davis, and Emmanuel LeRoy Ladurie share a common approach to history through court records. To varying degrees these scholars remain optimistic regarding the ability of criminal records to convey truth and meaning, but they differ in their assessment of the nature and extent of mediation in the documents. In his signature work, *Night Battles*, Carlo Ginzburg explains how the sixteenth-century Inquisition reconstructed the Friulian participants of a rural agrarian cult as diabolical witches.[39] Ginzburg relies on Inquisition transcripts that show this manipulation in action but remains confident in the ability of the records to "reach a genuinely popular stratum of beliefs." He notes that "the principal characteristic of this documentation is its immediacy" in spite of the testimonies having been translated from Friulian into Italian. "It is fair to say that the voices of these peasants reach us directly, without barriers, not by way, as usually happens, of fragmentary and indirect testimony, filtered through a different and inevitably distorting mentality."[40] Emmanuel LeRoy Ladurie, following Ginzburg, reveals a similar faith in the transparency of his early fourteenth-century records of the Inquisition against Albigensianism in the French Pyrenees. In *Montaillou*, LeRoy Ladurie demonstrates great certainty that the bishop's scribes provided an accurate Latin rendering of peasant testimonies originally delivered in Occitan.[41]

Finally, Natalie Zemon Davis in *Fictions in the Archives* artfully captures the narrative talents of ordinary folk who petitioned the sixteenth-century French king for a pardon.[42] Rather than an archive full of fiction, in the sense of untruth, Davis realizes the power of fiction, in the literary sense, to re-create the "rhetorical craft" and the mind of the time. She proceeds more carefully than Ginzburg or LeRoy Ladurie, accepting her documents at something less than face value. Davis acknowledges the limitations of her sources—for example, that the documents share formulaic similarities or use the third-person pronoun to recount first-person narratives. Relying on certain checks and balances on an individual's testimony (such as the fact-checking ability of the royal court or the existence of other statements and witnesses), Davis maintains that there is truth to be had among the archival "fictions." Her approach is instructive.

The archives from the Court of Aldermen share essential features and challenges with those court proceedings used by Ginzburg, LeRoy Ladurie, Davis, and others in terms of content, language, and form. Sentences and indictments handed down by the aldermen, especially regarding runaway slaves, could be as sermonic and didactic as any Inquisition document. Most statements from witnesses and defendants represent first-person accounts delivered in one language, then transcribed in the third person in another language. The aldermen maintained a multilingual staff of clerks who translated, on the spot, from Malay, Javanese, Chinese, Bugis, Portuguese, and so on into phonetic Old Dutch, or more correctly, phonetic Old Indies Dutch, as Asian loanwords peppered the eighteenth-century Dutch spoken in Batavia. When witnesses recounted important dialogues, court recorders often switched back into the original language in the documents, presumably to give a more literal rendering.[43] Familiar phrasing, procedures, and legalese in an interrogation's preface and conclusion, for example, serve as performative reminders of court ritual. The records of the Court of Aldermen are a singular source for the history of Southeast Asia, but commonalities with legal proceedings from other world regions should not be overlooked. We should share the optimism of historians writing history from crime but also their care, attentiveness, and attention to both big and little pictures.

Consequently, two separate but related projects are at work in this study. The first aim is to present a set of theoretical propositions, addressing a range of questions both "small" and "large." Smaller thesis-driven forays delve into topics such as the nature of gender and violence in Batavia or the creation of runaways in the colonial capital. Larger arguments about, for example, the interplay of demographics and economics with colonial law tie the smaller questions together. As a whole, this varied approach allows us to interpret populations as focused as the female underclass of Batavia or topics as broad as the legacy of gender and colonialism and the beginnings of the modern economic world system.

The second aim is recuperative. It is to rescue a few individuals from historical anonymity and partially reconstruct their lives for the reader. Heretofore, scholars have been at the mercy of the archives, and the little work done in the field tends to focus on the select groups of elite women who happen to appear in official Company archives, court poetry, or property struggles. Nothing approaching a life story has ever been written about a non-elite Southeast Asian woman from the early modern period. This should change. Records like those found in the Court of Aldermen, notarial archives, and church records not only name names but allow us to put a narrative face on a few individuals. Through them, we begin to understand what life was like for the multitude. In subsequent chapters, much ink is spent fleshing out quotidian details of these women's lives, wrapping a narration around the criminal event, an enterprise some readers might consider unnecessary or unrepresentative. Responding to this critique, it was Braudel who said, "the everyday happening is repeated, and the more often it is repeated the more likely it is to become a generality or rather a structure. It pervades society at all levels, and characterizes ways of being and behaving which are perpetuated through endless ages."[44]

2

ASIA TRADE AND
LIMITS OF THE POSSIBLE

Demographic and economic constraints underlay the Dutch presence in
Asia, coloring colonial society and the experience of Asian women with
Roman Dutch law. The ubiquity of interracial mixing between Europeans
and Asians because of the absence of European females pushed colonial officials to choose a legal system that discriminated based on VOC
employment and connection rather than on race. In short, this system
would not discriminate against the wives and sexual partners of VOC personnel. The economic realities of the age further buttressed this legal logic.
The VOC catapulted its wives (who once were slavinnen and concubines
or their offspring) into a position of legal privilege by treating them as
VOC employees in the eyes of the law. Conversely, for the women of the
underclass who never married into the VOC, their inclusion under the

umbrella of a dual legal system and the changing economic climate negatively impacted traditional forms of social advancement, pushing some slavinnen to take desperate measures.

DYING AND LIVING IN EARLY MODERN ASIA

Over the span of two centuries, from 1595 to 1795, almost a million men set sail for the East, departing from the Republic of the United Netherlands. Most left with the intention of returning home after making their fortunes in Asia, but as they would discover, returning to Europe after a Company stint of from three to five years was the exception rather than the rule. During that two-hundred-year period, less than one-third of the original million came home. The East Indies absorbed boatload after boatload of Company men as they intermarried into the local population, died of malaria, or both. Unlike many New World and settler colonies with a larger contingent of European women (until the nineteenth century), virtually all Europeans in Asia were men, and men who did not live long. Those lucky enough to survive tropical disease found it difficult to leave the East Indies with their fortunes intact—and impossible (that is, forbidden by the VOC) to return with their Eurasian families in tow.

An Asian wife, on the other hand, often fell heir to a legacy when a Company man fell victim to illness. Some of these women outlasted a succession of husbands and amassed impressive estates that became the object of ambitious suitors seeking a place in the Company elite.[1] In the midst of the transient European population, Asian women formed the heart of Indies society, both high and low, from the native nursemaids who raised Company men's children to the powerful heiresses who were courted by future governors general. To allow wealth to remain within Company families, hence within the Company, and to keep Asian Company wives from facing a different legal process, the VOC accorded them the same legal status as Dutch women upon marriage. Structural and demographic constraints—namely, distance and disease—kept the ratio of Europeans to Asians in the colonies very low. These forces entrenched interracial marriage and mixing as the norm in the social world of early modern Dutch Asia, impacting the lives of all Asian women there, women either with or without European legal status.

$\mathcal{W}$hen the Dutch first arrived at Jayakarta (as Batavia was known both before and after the Dutch interregnum), they did their best to re-create their European homeland.[2] Batavia had acquired its name from the storied, ancestral Dutch tribesmen living in the nether regions of northern Europe who, centuries earlier, were said to have fiercely resisted Roman imperialism. In 1619 a group of several hundred VOC soldiers bivouacked at Jayakarta, as the Company sought to create a headquarters for its operations in Asia. Under siege from the nearby sultanate of Banten, the Company began casting about for a symbol that would inspire hope and remind the troops of their birthplace. Under the circumstances, the name Batavia and its association with a heroic Dutch past made it the perfect symbol for their besieged headquarters. The VOC and Batavia's founder, Jan Pietersz Coen, initially conceived of the rendezvous as not only a trading base but also a settler colony. There, it was hoped, Europeans could seek to multiply their profit margins along with their numbers and culture—but the Company succeeded in only the first respect.

Who left Europe, bound for the East Indies? Between roughly 1600 and 1800, the VOC sent 978,000 men and a handful of European women to Asia. Aside from a few cross-dressing stowaways and an ill-fated shipload or two of Dutch maidens destined for Batavia (who turned out to be prostitutes), the VOC recruited only men. Although common soldiers made up the bulk of the East India Company rosters, some areas, South Africa in particular, had a small settler component that was large enough to be demographically significant. Such was not the case with the Southeast Asian destinations, however. Settlers often brought wives and families; soldiers did not. The transportation of European women to Asia remained altogether exceptional throughout the early modern period and remained distinctly uncommon until after the opening of the Suez Canal in 1869.[3]

The individuals in the settler communities such as the Cape of Good Hope were bound to much longer terms of service, sometimes fifteen years, and were better able to re-create the European societies from which they came. To this end, European women played a significant role. The settler versus soldier or sedentary versus sojourner dichotomy between the Atlantic settlements and the East Indies not only resulted in a certain cultural "apartheid" or island-of-Europeanness-in-the-wilderness mentality but also had the obvious demographic consequence that these European settler societies would be able to replicate themselves, both culturally and genetically. Both the proximity of the Americas to the Netherlands and the relatively temperate climate of the New World and the Cape were important factors in the conduciveness of these settler colonies to replicate themselves both culturally and genetically. Some VOC personnel finished out their term of service and became part of the *vrijburgher* (freeburgher) community. The Cape served as a refreshing station between Europe and Asia, and the VOC encouraged the freeburghers to till the soil and raise livestock. As trade relations soured between Capetown and Khoi Khoi pastoralists, a self-sustaining colony became essential.[4]

Between 1602 and 1795, for every hundred voyagers departing from Europe, seventeen died, deserted, or disembarked en route; forty-five lived, briefly, and died in Asia; five more disappeared en route back to Europe; a mere thirty-three limped back to Europe.[5] If a European passenger to Asia was fortunate enough not to die of scurvy on the long trip to the East Indies, he had to contend then with the host of local tropical diseases that claimed huge numbers of Europeans. A few led long lives and retired in Asia, but most succumbed to malaria, dysentery, or typhus.[6]

FATE OF THE VOC VOYAGER, 1602–1795

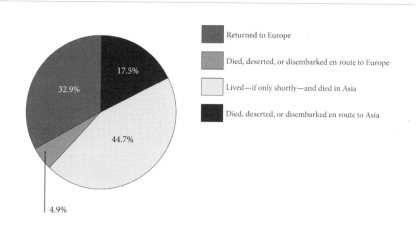

Of all VOC stations from South Africa to Japan, Batavia had the worst mortality rate by far. Research into death and disease in the colonies clarifies the grim state of public health for those VOC men who survived the rigors of the voyage to Asia. Eighteenth-century mortality rates for regular VOC employees who died after arrival in Asia (that is, not onboard ship) were five times as high as for adult males in Europe. Mortality rates for VOC soldiers were as much as ten times that of their counterparts in Europe. In the seventeenth century, visitors commented on Batavia city's health and beauty, but by the eighteenth century visitors described it as a "death pit." Batavia came to be widely regarded as a graveyard for Europeans and one of the most insalubrious cities in the world. In 1768–1769, a year for which comparative VOC mortality rates exist, Batavia lost 36 percent (1,995 out of 5,490) of its VOC servants. Even by local standards, the picture of public health in Batavia was not inviting. As a percentage, mortality rates were in the teens and twenties for other posts on Java and in the single digits for Eastern Indonesia. Contemporary urban Europe experienced something like a 3 percent annual adult mortality rate.[7] Why the change? What made Batavia so unhealthy?

Before 1733, the year the malaria epidemic began, 5–10 percent of the city's newcomers died within a year of their arrival, about the same mortality rate as other VOC stations. Then in the late 1720s, the governor general allowed Asian aquaculturists to begin construction on a network of *tambak*, or brackish fishponds, near the coast just north of Batavia's city center. The tambak produced for the city a harvest of a tasty herring-like fish called *bandeng*. Unfortunately, the tambak also provided an ideal breeding ground for the mosquito *anopheles sundiacus*, a ravenous malaria vector.[8] Carried by the bite of the female *anopheles sundiacus*, malaria began decimating Batavia's inhabitants in 1733 and continued to afflict the city well into the twentieth century. Coming out to feed between sunset and sunrise, *anopheles sundiacus* repeatedly exposed everyone within its two-kilometer-wide, sixty-centimeter-high flight path.[9] Sir Ronald Ross, 170 years later, discovered that malaria was carried by the female *anopheles* mosquito, but in the eighteenth century ideas and fears were somewhat less scientific. Observing that most people contracted "Batavian fever" (as it was then called) at night, people blamed the moonlight, the night wind, or Hippocrates' miasma.

Table 1

MORTALITY RATES FOR EUROPEAN VOC PERSONNEL,

FROM AUGUST 31, 1768, TO AUGUST 31, 1769

VOC Post	Mortality Rate
Batavia	36%
Java's North Coast	27%
Bantam	19%
Capetown	17%
Banda	16%
Palembang	11%
Cheribon	10%
Sumatra	9%
Ternate	9%
Bengal	8%
Banjermasin	6%
Melaka	6%
Ambon	6%
Timor	6%
Ceylon	5%
Malabar	5%
Coromandel	4%
Surat	4%
Makasar	4%
Japan	0%

Source: P. H. van der Brug, *Malaria en Malaise: De VOC in Batavia in de achttiende eeuw* (Amsterdam: De Bataafsche Leeuw, 1994).

So malaria became entrenched as a fact of life in Batavia, and newly arriving Europeans proved particularly susceptible to the disease. Before 1733, the VOC each day lost less than two of its personnel stationed in Batavia, a sustainable level of loss. Thereafter, deaths increased up to sixfold. From the beginning of the epidemic to the end of the eighteenth century, eighty-five thousand VOC personnel died in Batavia, mostly from malaria. Their numbers represent 20 percent of all who left Europe on VOC ships in the same period.

Asian and European alike, however, demonstrated vulnerability to malaria. The disease infected all newcomers equally, infants and immigrants, Asians and Europeans. Differing mortality rates for newly arriving Europeans and Asians may be only a question of uneven documentation. Anecdotal evidence suggests that Indian slaves and Javanese "mud coolies" (brought in to clean and unsilt the canals) contracted the disease as frequently as Europeans. Chinese migrants and infants fared no better. After 1733 roughly 50 percent of Batavian newcomers (men, women, and children) died within their first six months in the city. For those who survived their initial encounter with malaria, if they lived through nearly a decade of repeated exposure, they might finally acquire immunity to the disease, for acquiring natural immunity to malaria could require up to ten years. So, in order to survive Batavia, the newcomer had to endure a decade of repeated exposure to malaria and also survive dangerous secondary sicknesses such as dysentery and typhus.

One significant difference between Europeans and Asians in this malarial morass was that the disease was aggressively weeding out children born in Batavia. Those children who survived to adulthood were immune, while no such winnowing mechanism was acting on the adult newcomers from the Netherlands. This meant that if a Batavian-born woman married a newly arrived European, she would be immune because she had survived to adulthood. He, however, would have no immunity, and there would be a fifty-fifty chance that his bride would end up a widow in six months. Hence, high European mortality rates in tropical Asia shaped the demographic makeup of colonial settlements there.

Other European trading communities faced similar problems in areas where malaria, dysentery, and yellow fever were prominent.[10] The Portuguese, for example, suffered extremely high death rates in tropical Africa, which impacted the nature of their colonies there.[11] The New World differed from Asia and tropical Africa. Like British, French, Spanish, and Portuguese settlements in the Atlantic world, Dutch settlements in the Americas included European women; and like British, French, Spanish, and Portuguese settlements in the Asian world, the Dutch presence there was almost exclusively European male. However, it is not the case that the Dutch failed to encourage family settlement in Asia. In 1670 the ruling body of the VOC in the Netherlands, the Gentlemen XVII, offered "passage thence [to the Cape of Good Hope, Mauritius, Batavia, or Ceylon] on one of the ships of the Company without cost or tax, provided that [the settlers swear] an oath of allegiance to the said Company."[12] For most settlers this was not enough incentive for them to go to Asia and be swallowed up by tropical disease; it was, however, attractive enough for sailors and military recruits.

The VOC was the world's largest employer in the early modern period, and 978,000 of its personnel sailed to Asia between 1602 and 1795.[13] No other country or company came close to the numbers sent out in Dutch ships. From 1500 to 1800, the rest of Europe combined sent only 888,000 people to Asia.[14] Portugal then came in a distant second place with only 382,000. The Low Countries were uniquely positioned to supply so many hands. A fifteenth- and sixteenth-century downturn in arable farming caused by the overexploitation of peat and a shift toward less-labor-intensive livestock farming freed up masses of Dutch workers. They flocked to the urban centers, followed by the seventeenth- and eighteenth-century Germans and Eastern Dutch, giving the Netherlands a disproportionate number of medium-sized cities. The VOC promised the new urban migrants steady—if deadly—work, and droves of men came and died in Asia. As Fernand Braudel noted, "Can it not be said that there is a limit, a ceiling which restricts all human life, containing it within a frontier of varying outline, one which is hard to reach and harder still to cross? This is the border which in every age, even our own, separates the possible from the impossible, what can be done with a little effort from what cannot be done at all."[15] Distance and disease formed a barrier that the VOC was unable to cross en masse. Over the course of the seventeenth century, the VOC realized that intermarriage between its European agents and Asian women was the only viable option for maintaining a presence in Asia.

ECONOMICS OF THE ASIA TRADE

The VOC did not set out to expand and redirect Indonesian labor toward the bulk export of cash crops. Instead, the East India Company carefully contained and managed what was a small sector of the Asian economy, the spice trade. In 1492 Columbus had set sail for Indonesia, also known as the Indies, in search of cloves, nutmeg, mace, and other trade goods. Although headed in the direction of the Indonesian archipelago, Columbus ran ashore in the Caribbean, famously misnaming it the Indies and its inhabitants, Indians. Much is made of the "spirit of exploration" and the religious motivation behind his fateful voyage to the West Indies, but these key facts cannot be overlooked: he was headed for the East Indies or Indonesia, and it was the supply and demand for spices that animated his endeavor. In the days before refrigeration, the ability of fine spices to preserve and season perishable (not to mention bland) food, made them worth more than their weight in gold.[16] Until later transplantation, Maluku (the Spice Islands of Eastern Indonesia) was the only place in the world where these valuable products grew. Long before the Christian era, important stores of these fine spices had made their way to Europe via South and Southeast Asian maritime channels and Middle Eastern overland routes.[17] Beginning in the seventh century, the Southeast Asian kingdom of Srivijaya (centered in Palembang on Sumatra's east coast) became a hub of religious activity and trade between China and India, and of continued transshipping of fine spices and other bulk goods, primarily rice. Because of Srivijaya's disintegration, Melaka (located on the Malay peninsula across the Straits of Melaka from Palembang) emerged around 1400 as an important entrepot. Chinese, Arab, Indian, and Southeast Asian merchants flocked there, attracted to its impressive port facilities, fair legal system, and well-policed waterways.[18]

MELAKA AND MARITIME ASIA

Small-quantity high-value spices may have captured Europeans' imaginations and attracted them to Asia, but spices represented only a small part of Southeast Asian maritime commerce, a commerce that was much more than van Leur's "peddling trade." In terms of trade tonnage, bulk goods such as rice filled the holds of most merchant ships. Rice was not only a staple of Southeast Asian diets but also a staple of regional trade. It would be wrong, however, to think that spices were unimportant. As Anthony Reid points out, pepper and fine spices were of disproportionate significance because of the staggering profits they generated and because of the international mercantile attention they attracted.[19]

Melaka's fate provides a good example of both commerce in early modern Southeast Asia and the consequential role that spices could play. Melaka was the most important entrepot in the world before 1500, but its significance was largely a result of geography.[20] First, the Sunda Shelf is a shallow underwater extension of the Asian continent that connects Southeast Asia much in the same way the Mediterranean Sea connects the lands it defines. Abundant fisheries sustain life, and calm seas encourage traffic and intercourse. Violent eruptions are the tectonic result of the subduction of the Indian Australian Plate under the Sunda Shelf of the Eurasian Plate, a collision that also produces exceptionally fertile and life-sustaining volcanic soil. Second, moderate and reliable monsoon winds carried trade back and forth across the seas. During the summer months, warm air rising over the Asian landmass pulls winds northward off the cooler ocean while in winter the relatively warmer—and hence rising—ocean air forms a seat of low pressure, causing winds to blow to the south. Melaka was perfectly situated "below the winds" allowing Southeast Asian merchants to host traders from the shores of the Indian Ocean and those working the South China Sea.

From the Middle East and South Asia came Arabian coffee, Persian gold and raw silk, Malabar pepper, Gujarati and Coromandel indigo and textiles, Ceylonese cinnamon, and Bengalese textiles, raw silk, opium, saltpeter, and slaves. From East Asia came Cantonese tea, Chinese porcelain, and Japanese gold and copper. In addition to serving as a meeting place and market between the monsoons, Southeast Asia offered Burmese slaves and jars, Thai deer hides and forest products, Malayan tin, Cambodian rice and lacquer, Vietnamese silk and ceramics, and Indonesian gold, pepper, rice, forest products, and fine spices. The regularity of these seasonal monsoon winds and Melaka's strategic location offered a venue where the various players and products in the bustling Asian trade network could meet and traffic.[21] Asian merchants could spend the spring doing business in Melaka, the summer riding the winds back home to the northeast and northwest, the fall resupplying, and the winter traveling back to Melaka to start the cycle anew.

Adding to its impressive geographical endowment, the social and political arrangement of Melaka's human geography together formed an ideal mercantile climate. Emerging from the diaspora of an earlier Srivijayan merchant empire, Melaka's founder Parameswara came from Sumatra around 1400 and established another impressive trading state on those same straits. Srivijaya's foremost historian, Oliver Wolters, linked the rise and fall of that Sumatran empire to the ebb and flow of Chinese commercial interest and traffic to the area.[22] It should not surprise us then to learn that we can date Melaka's economic takeoff to the arrival of the enormous fleet of the Chinese admiral Zheng He in 1403. Parameswara agreed to Chinese vassalage in return for trading privileges and protection from the Thai. Ming emperor Chu Ti was interested in expanding trade in the Nanyang and sent seven maritime trade missions to Melaka over the next thirty years.[23] Official Chinese maritime activities ended abruptly in 1433 due to Mongol fears from the north, the expense of the missions, and a change in leadership, but the groundwork had already been laid for Melaka's success. Parameswara and his successors took further steps to encourage trade—policing the waterways for pirates, developing adequate port and warehouse facilities, and maintaining a fair and efficient judicial system—not the least of which was the adoption of Islam.

Beginning in the thirteenth century, Arab and Indian Islamic merchants (primarily Gujaratis) arrived and began making peaceful religious inroads at Pasai in northernmost Sumatra. Within the first decades after the founding of the port city, Melaka's royal family had converted to Islam, and Melaka was ruled by a commercial-minded sultanate. Islamic merchants from around the Indian Ocean sought out Melaka as a haven with familiar customs and an observant population. The *Sejarah Melayu*, a Melakan chronicle, details the fame, fortune, and influence to which Melaka aspired, and which in many ways it achieved. Long after the disappearance of the Melakan sultanate, that kingdom would—and for some still does—serve as a model for Malay courts and kingships elsewhere on the peninsula and across the archipelago.[24]

PORTUGAL AND THE SPICE FRENZY

In the beginning of the sixteenth century, Southeast Asia and Melaka in particular stood well positioned at the hub of a great Asian trading network. The Indonesian economy was sophisticated and outward-looking as many local farmers became specialized growers who tailored production to the global market and traded in kind and currency for their wants and needs instead of devoting their labors to subsistence agriculture.[25] A fraction of the spice trade—which trade was a fraction of the Asia trade as a whole—made its way to Europe, but the amounts were large enough to create widespread demand, and small enough to make a fortune for anyone who could increase the supply.

Portuguese traders were the first Europeans to attempt to bring the spices directly from Asia. Under the Portuguese prince Henry the Navigator, cadets from his maritime academy spent the fifteenth century groping their way down Africa's west coast, hugging the shore as they went.[26] Desperate to find their own route to Asia, the Portuguese under Vasco da Gama reached India in 1498, heard stories of the incredible entrepot on the Malay peninsula, and immediately began making plans to advance to Melaka where the biggest fortunes were to be made. Remarkably, given the two-year turnaround for a roundtrip from Europe to Asia, the Portuguese made it to Melaka by 1509. Their surprise attack was foiled by the Javanese lover of one of the Portuguese sailors, but in 1511 Afonso de Albuquerque returned to Melaka with more troops and superior firepower, and "Mighty Melaka" fell.

Portuguese greed, their distrust of the Chinese, and their crusade against Islam quickly turned Melaka into a mercantile backwater. While this was a blow to a once great city and the beginning of a permanent European presence in Southeast Asia, the Asian trading network was able to reconstitute itself elsewhere as traders congregated in north Sumatra and on Java's *pasisir* (mercantile north coast). The Portuguese quickly realized that capturing Melaka in no way translated into control of the spice trade. In the first place, clove, nutmeg, and mace production was decentralized and scattered across tiny family gardens in tiny Malukan islands and could not be controlled by sacking a fortress or conquering a city. Second, in exchange for spices, the growers demanded various products from the Asian market such as stylized Coromandel textiles, Chinese porcelain, and Javanese rice.

The fall of Melaka to the Portuguese was but a temporary setback for the spice trade. An important barometer of Portuguese ineffectiveness in controlling this lucrative trade was the caravan trade, which brought spices on their final leg of the journey through the Levant and into Europe—that is, not through Portuguese hands. Danish historian Niels Steensgaard has successfully shown that the caravan trade saw an initial reversal immediately following the entry of the Portuguese onto the Asian market but quickly rebounded, and that the caravan trade was performing at record levels by the end of the sixteenth century.[27] These caravans were fed by the Asian trade network that transshipped goods through regional emporia, and these emporia saw an increase in traffic as merchants chose new ports of call instead of Melaka. Like the caravan trade, the Portuguese disrupted maritime trade at the beginning of the sixteenth century, but again like the caravan trade, maritime trade recovered quickly and experienced a boom in the "long" sixteenth century. The Southeast Asian trading states of Ayutthaya, Aceh, Banten, and Makassar all had risen to unprecedented heights by the beginning of the seventeenth century. Their newfound wealth was founded upon rapid commercial buildup, and rulers poured their revenues into cannons, soldiers, and warships, increasing their power but also increasing the monopolistic and absolutist tendencies of these states as they scrambled to remain competitive with the VOC.[28]

The fundamental flaw with the Portuguese enterprise in Asia, the *Estado da India*, was its inability to maintain a consistent supply of pepper and spices to Europe, which kept prices far too high and inconsistent and made it worth the risk to the Estado's European rivals to compete directly for the spice trade. Given their commercial weakness, the Portuguese resorted to the conquest of a few ports along traditional trade routes, and instead of moving the goods on their own ships (thus incurring the risks but also the rewards), they collected taxes and customs from passing ships and granted passes (*cartazes*). The Estado da India has been described as little more than a "redistributive enterprise," existing on "tribute levied, not by virtue of its own productive activity."[29] Monopoly would have meant the end of the Estado da India; it relied on the tolls collected from Asian vessels, and the Portuguese were not in a position to carry much of the spices on their own. Spices continued coming onto the European market sporadically throughout the sixteenth century. Their price skyrocketed both because of this weak elasticity of supply and also because of the countless markups each time the goods changed hands from producer to consumer. High spice prices made it worth the gamble for Columbus and da Gama to strike out for the Indies, but Portuguese short-term profit seeking failed to meet European demand.[30] Essentially, the Estado da India brought no structural change to the spice trade or to the Asia trade, and the same incentives that brought the Portuguese at the beginning of the sixteenth century remained intact at the end of the century. The door was left open for European competitors to intervene, and the Dutch were in the perfect situation to do so.

MONOPOLY INC.— THE VOC AND COMPANY COLONIZATION

Dutch merchants had dominated European waterways since the fifteenth century, beating out their competition by providing low-cost transportation throughout Europe for bulk goods such as Baltic grain and North Sea herring.[31] The seventeenth century was a golden age for the Dutch Republic. Several historical factors contributed to Dutch ascendancy in Europe and Asia. In the absence of a truly feudal tradition and without a rigid society of orders fixed at birth, Dutch legal systems and power relationships allowed for a high level of social mobility.[32] Because power and wealth were not entrenched in an ancient aristocracy, the Dutch were unafraid of innovation, exploration, and changes to the status quo. Coupled with high urbanization, Dutch society produced atomized, independent individuals making rational choices in terms of their family, faith, and vocation—gesellschaft over gemeinschaft or, as de Vries and van der Woude wrote, "calculating instead of magical, individual instead of communal."[33] The Dutch economy witnessed trade primacy, high agricultural productivity, free (European) markets, and innovative yet stable financial institutions. The Dutch Republic guaranteed rights of property and contract, acted in the interests of merchants, managed its public finances well, at least until the 1670s, and took care of its waterways and its indigent.

By the turn of the seventeenth century, the Dutch shipping industry, buoyed by superior Dutch financial institutions and vast capital resources, was well positioned to dominate the Asia trade in a way the Portuguese never could. In the 1590s a Dutch sailor, Jan Huygen van Linschoten, who had been working under the Portuguese as the secretary of the bishop of Goa, published an extensive collection of reconnoitered maps, descriptions, and other information about the sea route from Europe to Maluku, technical information that formed the final piece in the puzzle of Dutch maritime dominance in the Indies. One year later, the first Dutch ship returned from Southeast Asia with a cargo of pepper and spices, a cargo that more than offset the sizeable losses suffered on the voyage. This touched off a Dutch "spice rush" to Indonesia, with independent Dutch venture capitalists sending sixty-five ships to Asia between 1595 and 1602, compared to only forty-six Portuguese ships in the same period. In 1602 the Dutch government under the leadership of Jan van Olden Barneveldt convinced competing spice firms to incorporate into a single trading company, the Verenigde Oost-Indische Compagnie (United Dutch East India Company). An economic juggernaut from a tiny land, the VOC proceeded to dominate European maritime trade and the Asian spice trade.

As the world's first multinational corporation, the VOC was truly a revolutionary institution that forever changed the way the West did business with rest of the world. An "institutional innovation," the VOC made important departures from previous forms of collective enterprise.[34] Foremost, the VOC was also the world's first joint stock company, and brokers traded its shares publicly on the Amsterdam exchange. Its significance for the development of capitalism cannot be overstated, but for the Asia trade, in particular, the VOC meant that, instead of a select group of merchants gambling their fortunes on the fate of an individual voyage to Asia, commercial risks would be shared among many shareholders and business strategy would be formulated over the long term. Previously, a few investors would buy, outfit, and underwrite an entire Asia-bound ship, pray for its success, and dissolve their capital stock, including ships, upon its return. Such a model did not encourage the development of a permanent fleet in Asia, the erection of all the necessary fortifications, and the commitment to long-range involvement in the region; the risks were simply too great and the rewards too belated for the small number of large investors.

The VOC was after the fine spices, but to get them, it had to participate in the intra-Asian trading network and become intimately involved in the region.[35] A brief description of VOC operations is a dizzying journey through the Old World. For example, Dutch East India ships sailed to

Asia with Spanish Peruvian silver as ballast, to exchange it in China for silk (and later, tea), in the meantime conquering Taiwan and establishing an office in Canton. The silk they exchanged in Japan for gold, copper, and Japanese silver. As the only Europeans allowed in Japan under the Tokugawa, they leased the island of Deshima, off the coast of Nagasaki. With precious metal, they purchased Indian textiles, built forts, and maintained a presence stretching all along the subcontinent, leasing no fewer than seventeen weaving factories and villages on the Coromandel coast alone (Pulicat, Jagannathapuram, Masulipatnam) to meet Southeast Asian demand. Finally, those textiles were traded on the Indonesian market for pepper and fine Maluku spices. This does not include the Company's massive operations elsewhere, including facilities in South Africa (a refreshing station), Yemen (coffee in al-Mukha,), Iran (sugar for silk in Bandar Abbas on the Strait of Hormuz), and Pakistan (taking textiles from Sind). From Gujarat came indigo; from Dutch-conquered Sri Lanka came cinnamon. Company factors in Bengal and Burma traded for slaves and, later, earthen jars. Thailand produced deer hides and forest products, and tin was mined on the Malay peninsula, all brokered through VOC agents. Udong (on Cambodia's lake Tonle Sap) and Laos brought forth rice and lacquer while Vietnamese VOC lodges at Pho Hien in the north and Hoi An along the central coast dealt in silk, ceramics, and porcelain, among other things. Therefore, with a small investment in silver, the Company was able to increase its earnings significantly as it profited with each transaction along the Asian trading network.

The intra-Asia trade enriched Company coffers, but in the early years of the VOC, the profits of 1,000 percent and more came only from cloves, nutmeg, and mace. Once in Asian waters, the VOC began to move aggressively to corner the market in these spices. As Els Jacobs stated, "[the] building up of the Asian trading network was done for no other reason than the spice trade."[36] In pre-Company days, Dutch concerns had produced huge profits for their investors, and in order to guarantee the kind of return expected by VOC stockholders the Company needed to control the spice trade. The Company took a twofold approach. First, of obvious importance was controlling the production of clove, nutmeg, and mace at their source in Eastern Indonesia. Second, from their experience in the pre-monopoly days, the Dutch knew that controlling the sites of spice production did not necessarily mean controlling spice traffic, and so they also went after rival centers of trade.

Controlling spice production meant controlling Maluku, as cultivation of fine spices was limited to that region of Eastern Indonesia. Cloves were endemic to the tiny islands of Ternate, Tidore, Moti, Makian, and Bacan in the north; and the island of Banda, further south, was home to nutmeg and mace. The Portuguese had failed at their attempt at monopoly but were at least successful in maintaining a presence in the Malukan political seat of Ternate—but only with the help of neighboring Tidore and Spanish Manila, with whom the Portuguese worked closely following the unification of the Iberian crown in 1580. By 1607 the Dutch had an outpost on Ternate and were bent on monopolizing the whole of the trade. Although VOC fleets roamed the waters, they were unable to prevent what they defined as smuggling (what we would define as free trade), so they resorted to a policy of eradication or extirpation (*extirpatie*) in 1652. All clove production was moved to Ambon, which had been conquered from the Portuguese in 1605, was more firmly under Dutch control, and had a loyal Christian *burgerij*. Then the VOC destroyed the clove trees elsewhere in the archipelago. In return for their participation and policing, the Company offered compensatory stipends (and perpetual dependence) to the sultanates of the former clove islands. The residents of the Banda Islands were less willing to relinquish control over their nutmeg and mace industry. VOC patrols repeatedly found Bandanese merchants "guilty" of selling nutmeg and mace at fair price on the open market to Asian and European competitors. In retaliation, Batavia's founder Jan Pieterszoon Coen ordered the removal of the peoples of the Banda Islands in 1621. He replaced them with slaves and loyal Dutch and Indonesians who would sell only to the Company at a fixed price. The wiping out of the nutmeg- and mace-growing population of the Bandas tightened the Dutch grip on the area, and the mid seventeenth-century acknowledgment of Dutch suzerainty by the North Malukan cradle of clove production increased VOC control to a virtual stranglehold. Further mopping-up campaigns of "renegade" spice cultivators were complete by the 1670s when the spice monopoly was finally in hand.

Eliminating rival trading centers was also an important part of the Dutch strategy of controlling prices by controlling supply. Although 130 years of not untypical Portuguese mismanagement had reduced Melaka to a mere specter of its former status as the world's greatest entrepot, the

Table 2

EIGHTEENTH-CENTURY TRADE BETWEEN VOC STATIONS

VOC Station	Export Items	Import Items
Ambon (Maluku)	Cloves, textiles	Silver, textiles, gold
Banda (Maluku)	Nutmeg, mace	Silver, textiles, gold, sugar
Ternate (Maluku)	Silver, gold	Silver, textiles, gold
Makassar (Sulawesi)	Silver, slaves, brazilwood	Silver, textiles, gold, coffee
Timor	Silver, gold	Silver, textiles, gold
Ceylon (Sri Lanka)	Silver, cinnamon, pepper, textiles, saltpeter, Japanese copper, gold, tin	Silver, cloves, nutmeg, mace, pepper, textiles, raw silk, saltpeter, opium, Japanese copper, gold, tin, sugar, coffee
Jambi (Sumatra)	Pepper, gold	Silver, textiles
Palembang (Sumatra)	Silver, pepper, tin	Silver, textiles
Banten (Java)	Pepper	Silver, textiles, gold
Malabar (SW India)	Silver, cinnamon, pepper, textiles, saltpeter, Japanese copper, gold	Silver, cloves, nutmeg, mace, textiles, saltpeter, Japanese copper, gold, tin, sugar
Banjermasin (Borneo)	Silver, pepper, gold, tin	Silver, textiles
Coromandel (SE India)	Silver, textiles, Japanese copper, gold	Silver, cloves, nutmeg, mace, pepper, textiles, saltpeter, Japanese copper, gold, tin, sugar, coffee
Surat (NW India)	Silver, cinnamon, pepper, textiles, Japanese copper, gold, sugar	Silver, cloves, nutmeg, mace, cinnamon, pepper, Japanese copper, tin, sugar
Bengal	Pepper, textiles, raw silk, salt peter, opium (to Batavia), Japanese copper	Silver, cloves, nutmeg, mace, cinnamon, pepper, Japanese copper, gold, tin, sugar, coffee
Cochin-China (Mekong, Vietnam)	Gold, sugar	Silver, saltpeter, Japanese copper

Table 2 continued

EIGHTEENTH-CENTURY TRADE BETWEEN VOC STATIONS

VOC Station	Export Items	Import Items
Japan	Textiles, raw silk, Japanese copper, gold	Silver, cloves, pepper, textiles, raw silk, tin, sugar
Basra (Persia, Iraq)	Silver, raw silk, gold	Cloves, nutmeg, mace, cinnamon, pepper, textiles, raw silk, tin, sugar, coffee
Padang (Sumatra)	Pepper, gold	Silver, textiles
Pontianak (Borneo)	Gold	Silver
Canton	Textiles, raw silk, gold, sugar	Silver, cloves, nutmeg, pepper, Japanese copper, tin
Melaka (Malaysia)	Silver, textiles, Japanese copper, gold, tin	Silver, fine spices, cinnamon, pepper, textiles, raw silk, saltpeter, opium, Japanese copper, gold, sugar
Siam (Thailand)	Gold, tin	Silver, textiles, sugar
Batavia (Java)	Silver, cloves, nutmeg, mace, raw silk, saltpeter, Japanese copper, gold, tin sugar, coffee	Silver, cloves, nutmeg, mace, cinnamon, pepper, textiles, raw silk, saltpeter, opium, Japanese copper, gold, tin, sugar, coffee
Cheribon (Java)	Pepper, sugar, coffee	Silver, textiles, tin
Semarang (Java)	Silver, pepper, textiles, sugar, coffee	Silver, textiles, Japanese copper, gold
Mocha (Yemen)	Silver, cloves, textiles, gold, coffee	Silver, cloves, nutmeg, mace, pepper, textiles, Japanese copper, gold, tin, sugar
Cape of Good Hope (South Africa)	Silver, textiles	Silver, textiles, sugar, coffee

Source: Els M. Jacobs, *Koopman in Azië: De handel van de Verenigde Oost-Indische Compagnie tijdens de 18de eeuw* (Zutphen: Walburg Pers, 2000), 230–46.

Dutch still felt it necessary to control traffic in the Straits of Melaka, and they drove the Portuguese out of the Malay peninsula in 1641. Although the VOC had eradicated most of the clove trees outside of Dutch Ambon, the scattered home-based nature of North Malukan clove cultivation made it difficult to police any rogue growers. The VOC paid informants and sent out tree patrols, but cloves continued to trickle out of Ternate, Tidor, and the surrounding islands. Even the new VOC transplants to the Bandas "illegally" sold to non-VOC merchants, and black market cloves, nutmeg, and mace continued to show up in Asian entrepots such as Makassar on Sulawesi. Unwilling to tolerate such a circumvention of its monopoly, the VOC teamed up with Arung Palakka and the Bugis—excellent sailors and enemies of the kingdom of Gowa, which ruled Makassar—to defeat the South Sulawesi metropolis in 1667. The Company enforced a ban on all foreign traders to what had hitherto been the region's biggest center for "illegal spice traffic," Makassar.[37]

Pepper, which grew all around Indonesia and on India's Malabar Coast, was nearly impossible to control at its source, and so the most effective means of regulating its supply to the European market was to contain rival entrepots. Aceh in North Sumatra was a major pepper emporium for the world and hence a problem to the VOC. The Company went after its suppliers, and by 1670 the pepper-producing west coast of Sumatra and the Sumatran tin districts had been wrested from Acehnese suzerainty. Banten, just west of Batavia, was a double threat as a pepper hub and a haven for the English. Overlapping claims to Banten's hinterlands sent the VOC willingly into a showdown with Banten's sultan Ageng. War and a resulting succession crisis provided the VOC with a division they could exploit, and Banten was reduced to vassalage by 1684.[38]

Statistically, the VOC eclipsed all its rivals in the Asia trade. In its two-century lifespan from 1602 to 1799 the VOC sent almost a million people to work in the Asia trade (the rest of Europe combined sent only 882,412 people from 1500 to 1795) on 4,785 ships (England was a distant second with 2,690 ships) and returned with more than two and a half million tons of Asian trade goods (five times the tonnage of their closest competitor).[39] Even in its ascendancy, the Company had to perform a careful balancing act. European demand for black pepper, cloves, nutmeg, mace, and cinnamon was only relatively inelastic because of the small amounts used and the limited number of their applications in cosmetics and medicines, seasonings and preservatives. But the VOC was an institutional innovation over the Portuguese Estado da India, and the Dutch were able not only to participate in the Asia trade but also to monopolize the spice trade. In the end, being in charge meant manipulating the supply of spices to the European market. In addition to controlling the centers of spice production and conquering Asian entrepots, the Company devised an interesting strategy to ensure medium- and long-term profits and discourage European rivals. To prevent extra-VOC trading in Europe, the Company warehoused around ten times more than market demand of the spices and guaranteed a rock steady, artificially high but not exorbitant price for their product. From 1680 and for decades thereafter, 3.75 guilders per pound was the European price at which the VOC sold cloves and nutmeg, a gross profit of 1,400 percent and 7,400 percent respectively.[40]

The traffic in fine spices and pepper—a monopoly based on securing scarcity—was not served by the plantation system. Instead the VOC commercial empire was based on controlling the sites of production and artificially fixing world supply and prices such that it was dear enough to secure long-term profits but not so dear that others would vie for it at all costs. In such a scenario, the Dutch had no interest in cultivating vast tracts of land for the spice trade but instead kept a close watch on its limited acreage. The nature of this very important economic distinction between the early and late modern periods was important. Its uniqueness allowed, along with the demographic picture before 1800, the early colonial state to take a pragmatic approach by promulgating a universal law code. And if Dutch colonialism was nothing else, it was pragmatic.

Indeed, pragmatism in the pursuit of profits was at the heart of VOC activity. The results were sometimes shocking and brutal, but the lust for lucre also led the VOC down some surprisingly enlightened and progressive avenues, by contemporary standards.[41] Unlike the British who were incessantly preoccupied with racial purity and cultural contamination in their colonies, throughout the seventeenth, eighteenth, and most of the nineteenth centuries, the Dutch cohabited and intermarried with the Asian community simply because racial mixing was more practical and realistic, given the virtual absence of European women making the early modern voyage to Asia. And so, greed was tempered by a desire for sustained growth, and it led the VOC into unique and seemingly contradictory situations—for sometimes tolerance paid, and sometimes it did not. If marrying a local woman was what was required to create a network within a local economy, there were no misgivings about mixed marriages, but if exterminating the urban Chinese (as happened in 1741 in Batavia) was necessary to preserve Company hegemony, then ethnic cleansing was deemed necessary. If treaties could monopolize the delivery of trade goods, then friendly alliances would be made with sultanates and princedoms, but if an island refused to cooperate, it might be razed and its inhabitants slaughtered (as happened on Banda in 1641).[42]

Even though the Company became more widely and directly involved in Asian affairs in the course of the eighteenth century, its fortunes did not yet rest squarely on the backs of the millions of common Indonesians who would buttress the nineteenth-century colonial state. Producing vast quantities of fine trade goods, which would have required much more direct control over large numbers of Indonesians, went against the VOC's business strategy. Instead, the Company destroyed its rivals, kept close watch over the sites of production, and controlled European prices by manipulating market supply there. In the early modern period, the Dutch administered only small parts of Java and scattered enclaves in the Outer Islands.

*T*he following photos are rare ethnographic images from nineteenth-century
Batavia. Though the settings are staged, the
gaze is voyeuristic, and these individuals
are not contemporaries with those in
Wives, Slaves, and Concubines, they do
capture a slice of urban life from the
colonial capital.

Stadhuis Batavia, the courthouse where the proceedings of the criminal trials were held.

Well-dressed Asian women pose with jewelry and fine clothes.

Elements of Asian and European style co-mingle.

Two Japanese
women pose in their
traditional dress for
the camera and for
posterity. Note the
artistic reflection of
the woman's face in
the mirror.

A couple in wedding attire.

Two scenes from domestic life: weaving and caring for the children.

A young Indonesian woman dances to music provided by indigenous musicians.

(above) A young girl poses in beautiful batik.

(right) A young woman poses in a Victorian-style environment.

(above) A young woman poses provocatively for the photographer.

(right) A young woman wearing a batik dress stands in a contrived native setting.

A series of voyeuristic photographs objectifying young Asian women.

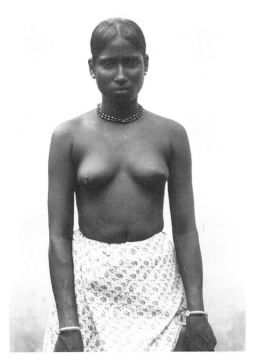

Vignettes from
"everyday life":
sewing, chopping
coconuts, and hang-
ing clothes.

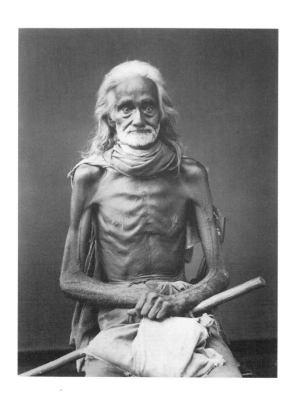

(above) Emaciated,
elderly man.

(right) Two women
pounding grain.

(next page) A young
woman balances a
fruit basket on her
head.

COURTS AND COURTSHIP

Legal Practice in Dutch Asia

The Dutch East India Company took an innovative and deliberate approach to the Asian trade network. It made huge capital investments in Asia with extended long-term planning. It monopolized the supply chain, and so on, and this all influenced its rise to preeminence. But there is another aspect that is vital in explaining Company operations and behaviors, and perhaps this is the most central organizing principle to the Dutch East India Company—pragmatism, the principle without principles.

The Company constructed a local legal framework in its Southeast Asian territories around two important considerations: the desire to protect and promote VOC employees and their mostly Asian dependents and the ability to discriminate—not by race but by Company or non-Company status—against their European rivals, namely, the British. The pragmatism that animated the Company approach to colonial law also conditioned the VOC's response to the demographic and economic forces defining its jurisprudence. One of the most important consequences of this melding of VOC pragmatism with structural realities was the creation of a legal underclass. VOC law codes—and the categories they created—came to construct concrete categories out of a hitherto flexible and sliding social scale.

DEFINING DUTCH COLONIAL LAW

The colonial law codes, which would morph and reshape to conform to the realities of life in Southeast Asia, were themselves born out of a rich tradition of legal melding of code with custom. This heritage of legal hybridization no doubt set a precedent for juridical practice overseas. *Roomsch-Hollandsch Recht* (Roman Dutch law) was the legal system that obtained, to varying degrees, in the provinces of the Netherlands and their colonies in the early modern period, until it was replaced by the *Franse Wetgeving* (Napoleonic Code) in 1810. As its name implies, Roman Dutch law is an amalgam of several legal traditions. In the sixth century A.D. Justinian, the ruler of the Byzantine empire, codified the body of Roman law into what became known as the *Corpus Juris Civilis* (Justinian's Code), which represented the institutionalization of a thousand years of Roman legal practice and juridical thought. By at least the twelfth century, Justinian's Code was studied seriously in Europe's universities and formed the civil law corpus for European jurists. In late medieval and early modern Northern Europe, countries began using Roman law and Canon law to augment Germanic customary legal traditions.[1]

During the fifteenth and sixteenth centuries in much of the area that is today the Netherlands, Roman law was gradually incorporated into Dutch jurisprudence, hence Roman Dutch law. Under French Burgundian and especially under Spanish Hapsburg rule in the Netherlands, university-trained jurists in Roman law began supplementing the Germanic code with the Roman one.[2] This was the most important function of Roman law in early modern Europe.[3] Parts of the Roman statutory canon could be cannibalized as needed, and many legal texts in both the Netherlands and their colonies stated that where local law and custom fell short or were silent, the Roman law was to be followed.[4] In Dutch-controlled Asia, the very pliability of the Roman Dutch law would allow it to be molded and adapted to local needs and circumstances and the twice-hybridized colonial law—Roman law with Dutch custom and the resulting Roman Dutch law with Asian custom—was a useful instrument for dealing with the hybridized mestizo world of the VOC.

THE LEGAL FOUNDATIONS OF
THE FEMALE ELITE IN DUTCH ASIA

A fundamental reality of life in the Indies, and a reality that was reflected in the law code, was the absence of European women. For the Company and the colony to survive, Dutch men in Southeast Asia began taking long-term Asian wives and mistresses. From the beginning of the seventeenth century, demographic idiosyncrasies subordinated a concern with race as the Dutch developed their social and conceptual categories. Widespread interracial cohabiting forced the Dutch to adopt more fluid, non-race-based markers of difference.

Throughout the first decades of its existence the VOC, founded in 1602, sought both a practical and a juridical solution to its demographic problem. Several early seventeenth-century attempts to bring over European women failed miserably. Without the presence of Dutch women, the East India Company came to realize, its initial notion of a homogenous European colony would have to be expanded, and its notion of marriage as an institution confined to European Christians would have to be ignored. For the colony to work, the native companions of Company men had to be included in the equation. But the Company wanted more than just intimate partners for its men; it wanted the permanence of stable married family units.

Early VOC contests and confrontations with the Portuguese in Asia informed the Dutch attempt to construct society. VOC officers had witnessed firsthand the fierce resistance put up by the mestizo Portuguese Asian populations of Ambon (1605), Macau (1622), and Melaka (1641) as the VOC laid siege. The heavy-handed religious admonitions behind the proclamation on marriage were used as strong-arm tactics by the VOC to encourage its men to marry their concubines, who then became wives who produced a loyal citizenry. An important long-term goal of the Company was to create a *burgerschap* that could be counted on in times of siege. When the initial

Dutch attempts at building a pure European colony were thwarted, they quickly adapted to the so-called Portuguese model of easy racial mixing. Like the Portuguese, the VOC would try to compensate for its failure to replicate "Europe" demographically by its desperate attempts to replicate itself culturally in the lives of the Asian women pairing up with Dutch men.

Although the VOC eventually came around to the idea of interracial marriage, it had from the very outset railed aggressively against extramarital relations. Coinciding with the cessation of Dutch female immigration was the Company's first of many statements against the keeping of concubines. Promulgated on 11 December 1620, this short edict outlawed concubinage for two interesting reasons: the first was "the all too lamentable and familiar examples of aborting the fetus or the one concubine trying to murder the other with poison," and the second was "as much as possible to keep God's wrath away from this republic."[5] An edict, published eighteen months later, more fully explained this fear of God's wrath. This extended set of VOC directives on concubinage, promulgated in 1622, came in large part because of the nonobservance of earlier warnings (including the 1620 warning) to Company men of all ranks.

The heading of the 20 July 1622 edict against concubinage addressed both the failure of the rank and file to comply with previous edicts and the blatant indifference shown by Company officials toward the enforcement of the law. It cited the "lack of restraint by the inhabitants or the non-pursuance [of the law?] by the negligence of officers, over the course of time," as the motivating factor in the administration's decision to reissue a statement on the matter. This was not only a problem that the lower rungs of the Company hierarchy became involved in; the keeping of concubines was a widespread practice from the highest administrative levels on down. Accordingly, the edict began with the caveat that concubinage would be punished "regardless of what place or position the guilty [party] be under our jurisdiction." Issued as a "renovation and amplification of ordinances and edicts regarding concubinage, adultery and incest," the 1622 law marked concubinage as deviant, placing it under the larger umbrella covering adultery and incest. Literally described as "mixing oneself [*zich vermengelen*] with a slave or free woman," sex and concubinage were broken down into two distinct orders—relations between those of the same faith and relations between those of different faiths. So long as the infidelity was intra-faith, punishments for solicitation were mild and left to the discretion of the court: "Attempts at concubinage, those dishonorably soliciting a woman or treating scandalously, are punished according to the situation and as the judge sees fit." We might compare this to the severity of the punishment for sexual relations between Christian and non-Christian: "the judge may punish, 'bodily or in property or both,'" the Christian man or the Christian woman who "is lost in simple fornication or concubinage with a Moor, Pagan or other." The non-Christian "instigator or initiator to the transgression committed is punished with death."[6]

Following the statutes that delineated what constituted a sex crime and what its respective punishment should be, the 1622 code offered a lengthy proclamation about the sanctity of marriage. Filled with prophecies of doom and gloom for adulterous nations, the proclamation broke with the generally secular tone of most Company legal discourse and lamented the "all-destructive curse of the Lord" that hangs over the peoples who practice "dishonest union[s], hated concubinage and God-grieving adultery." The code described the institution of marriage as the "only nursemaid of human happiness," idealized by the proclamation as the "utmost and absolute necessity . . . in well-to-do republics and in all States." Marriage, not concubinage, would be the answer to Company problems.[7]

By the time the Dutch had established a foothold in Asia, state control over marriage in the Netherlands and the issuing of marriage proclamations were common practice, but colonial controls on marriage initially differed substantially from the Roman Dutch. As part the VOC's effort to establish a loyal *burgerschap* in Dutch Asia, the church retained control over marriage longer in the colonies than it did in Europe. In the metropole, the Dutch Reformed Church had "lost" control over marriage to the state since 1578, but in Dutch Asia the Reformed Church Council continued responsible for registering marriage proclamations until 1632. A 1621 colonial law prohibited "marriage and baptism without . . . consent and recommendation from our respective authorities of this place." The law continued that consent and recommendation, "from the servants of God's holy word, thereto authorized by the parish of the holy church of the United Netherlands and permitted by us" with a fine of fifty pieces of eight and punishment at the court's discretion.[8]

Worries about the true nature of the conversion of Asian women to the Dutch Reformed faith ran throughout later edicts, but these proclamations also voiced a deeper concern about the conversion of Asian women to Dutch culture. In effect, marriage proclamations became a cultural gatekeeper, policing the "Dutchness" of Company brides. In 1632 a directive to the Court of Aldermen in Batavia set up Commissioners of Matrimonial Affairs, paralleling that institution in the Netherlands. Until this directive, the difference in marriage between the Netherlands and Dutch Asia might seem to have arisen only because of an institutional time lag between the Dutch state and its colonial concerns, but as the 1632 marriage proclamation and subsequent edicts demonstrate, the colonial state had an additional set of concerns, namely, interracial marriage of newly converted Asian women to Calvinist men. Moreover, the 1632 directive required permission from the governor general for Company personnel to register a marriage proclamation. And there was an additional "spiritual" requirement, conspicuously absent from laws promulgated in the Netherlands. "Blacks [*swarten*]," it read, also could not register a marriage proclamation unless they were "furnished with an attestation, granted by the church council, to the effect that they were 'instructed substantially in the first principles of the Christian religion.'"[9]

The nominal use of the Dutch language in Asia deeply concerned the *Hoge Regering* (High Government). As time passed, the ability to speak Dutch became a vital requirement for Company brides, providing a preeminent marker of Dutchness. A 1641 edict claimed that "the use of the Portuguese language had expanded so much in Batavia and in other Company stations that the government foresaw '[the Portuguese language] gaining the upper hand and smothering, once and for all, the language of our fatherland.'"[10] The edict also blamed the slaves for it. One of the "means to the advancement of the knowledge and the use of the Dutch language" was to disallow "native women, 'who do not moderately speak and understand our Dutch language'" to marry Dutch men.[11] The Commissioners for Matrimonial Affairs were to act as a sort of language board, giving out certificates of language competency for marriages and other purposes. Their language-monitoring function was repeated in the 1642 statutes of Batavia: "For sound reasons, the aforementioned commissioners are henceforth expressly forbidden to register a marriage proclamation of a Netherlander with any native woman unless she can moderately understand and speak the Dutch language."[12]

$\mathcal{B}$y the middle of the seventeenth century, then, the VOC had established a legal system that legitimated the relationships formed by Company men with Asian women, creating in Southeast Asia an institution of Dutch Asian marriage. In order to gain economic advantage, trading states (European and Asian alike) were willing to overlook differences of race, religion, and culture that would become so insurmountable in later centuries. The wives of Company employees were the immediate beneficiaries of the colonial marriage law. Once married, Company wives gained full European status, access to special VOC courts, and the same relatively progressive legal, especially inheritance, rights as Dutch women.

High European mortality generated Dutch Asian marriage, but it also forced the Company to consider the fate of the offspring of those unions, especially those left as orphans when their Dutch fathers succumbed to tropical disease. In the statutory sense, there was no discernable difference between the Netherlands and its colonies regarding orphans (*weeskinderen*) or the orphanage (*weeskamer*).[13] This was only in the statutory sense. In practice, the high mortality of European men made orphanhood a larger issue in the Indies. The primary concern was capital flight. If a VOC employee died with no wife and no heirs other than an illegitimate orphan child, family back in the Netherlands might claim his Asian holdings and insist upon their repatriation. A statement in the 1642 statutes of Batavia instructing the weesmeester pointed to this problem: "Daily in these lands many people die who leave behind no kin or heirs who should receive their property, and that said property usually would be squandered and come to nothing."[14] The Company was interested in creating a viable citizenry in Asia, and remittances and asset liquidation in the Indies worked against this end. This made the case for marriage all the more important. By recognizing mixed marriages and granting Asian women Dutch legal status, the VOC was better able to ensure that the personal wealth accumulated in Batavia would remain in Batavia.

In the case of the Indies, the Roman Dutch law fit seamlessly with the significant role that Asian women would play in the commercial realm.

In existing Southeast Asian trade relations, temporary marriage played a critical role. Under these arrangements, a monsoon-riding merchant could empower a local woman to run his business while he was away. For instance, she could buy and sell his property, establish relationships with spice brokers, and generally look after his commercial affairs. Similar relationships had developed in the Netherlands. Grotius explained how this early modern businesswoman came into existence. According to our jurist, "in times of old" a woman was allowed to indebt her husband up to four pennies on household goods, but the husband was liable for no more. "But later, the commerce and wealth of the country being greatly increased, the principle was extended so that today a married woman engaged in public commerce or trade may contract in all matters relating thereto and consequently may bind herself and her husband and alienate and encumber her stock." In this way, women whose husbands publicly declared them as their business agents could "alienate or encumber her husband's property or her own."[15]

In both Roman Dutch and colonial statutes, edicts on marriage, legitimacy, and the welfare of children demonstrate how tightly woven social concerns were with economic considerations, illuminating the ways in which colonial Dutch law empowered women in the Dutch Asian elite. This was particularly conspicuous in the case of property and marriage. Under Roman Dutch law in the Netherlands, at the contraction of a marriage, the estates of husband and wife were brought together and held in common. This "community of goods" included both assets and liabilities. During the marriage debts and earnings applied to this common purse, and husband and wife shared equally in it if the marriage ended. Although the couple held marriage property in common, without her husband's consent a married woman "may not," wrote Grotius, "alienate or encumber her husband's property or her own; may not contract debts to bind herself or her husband."[16] The wife was able to buy food and household goods without her husband's consent, and with his additional blessing she could act as his full-fledged business agent.

In pursuit of the bottom line, the Company chose for interracial marriage and opted for the Portuguese-like model of easy racial mixing and integration. Given the constraints of distance and disease, the VOC had very few choices. At times, though not without frequent exception, early modern Dutch Asia looked very much like the place the post–World War II Netherlands *imagined* itself to be: a cosmopolitan island of racially tolerant prosperity.[17] These sentiments were contingent upon deeper material realities, and with the later nineteenth-century containment of malaria, the advent of the steamship, and the opening of the Suez Canal, the terrain shifted, and so did colonial affect. But until then, the demographic baseline and the nature of the early modern commercial enterprise would conspire to promote a legal system that was not race-based and that supported the VOC system.

THE LEGAL ORIGINS OF THE DUTCH ASIAN UNDERCLASS

The separation of the population into VOC and non-VOC was the most fundamental and most important legal distinction in the early modern Dutch colonies. Driven by competition and enabled by pragmatism, VOC law divided people into two kinds: those inside the Company and those outside the Company. Individuals employed by the VOC were given special treatment—including their own judicial system. For VOC personnel and their families and slaves, the Company established a separate court system, the *Raad van Justitie* (Council of Justice) with the *Advocaat-Fiskaal* (fiscal advocate) acting as chief prosecutor. This court served as a *forum privilegiatum* for the Company class. It was chaired by a member of the *Raad van Indië* (Council of the Indies) and staffed, in theory, by ranking Company men with legal training. As for the *burgerbevolking* (civilian population), European or Asian, their cases were heard together in the *Schepenbank* (Court of Aldermen). Although still under the governor general, this court was staffed by important Chinese and European civilians who were not necessarily legal professionals. The Court of Aldermen staff served double duty by running the local police force with the Justitie.[18] Of utmost importance, the Council of Justice was much better equipped than the Court of Aldermen to try complicated questions of inheritance and complex civil and criminal proceedings.

By fits and starts, the VOC eventually arrived at a legal system that reflected the economic values of the Company and that opened the door (which did not close until the late nineteenth century) for Asian and Eurasian women to dominate the early modern colonial social world.

Although important, the non-Company populations—whether native, foreign, Oriental, or European—were not given access to the Company courts. In many cases this put Asians, especially Asian women married to Company men, ahead of non-Company Europeans. Conversely, this legal system laid the foundations for an ethnically mixed underclass in Dutch Batavia. In the first instance, it closed off many traditional avenues for social advancement among the women of the lower class. As the legal system privileged those connected to the Company, it disadvantaged those who were not. Non-Company residents of the Dutch Asian capital—no matter their extraction, gender, or status—found their disputes relegated to the Court of Aldermen.

COMPANY ORGANIZATION AND VOC LAW

From 1595 to 1602, Dutch merchant syndicates competed fiercely in the Asia trade. Even during this mad scramble (referred to as the *wilde vaart*), Asia-bound Dutch ships had to carry three types of legal authorization.[19] The first was known as a *patent*. It was issued by Prince Maurits himself and granted diplomatic permission for the journey. Second, each ship's captain was given a *commissie*, which regulated the haul and served as his license to act in the capacity of captain. Finally, an *artikelbrief* stipulated for the sailors where the ship's laws deviated from standard Dutch law and mostly related to testaments and salaries. These documents granted the ships express authority to circumvent the Portuguese in Asia. In the pre-VOC period, some investors realized huge profits as they battled with fellow Dutchmen for a piece of the action.

These ad hoc grants of power might have proved useful for generating short-term profits but were bad for sustaining them in the long run. As a result, in 1602 the States General of the Netherlands persuaded competing East Indian trading firms to consolidate their resources and capital into the United Dutch East India Company. They granted the VOC a charter that was subject to renewal by the States General in twenty-one years. Dutch cities with significant East Indies firms formed chambers that were given proportional representation in the ruling body of the Company in the Netherlands, the *Heren XVII* (Gentlemen XVII). Until the appointment of a Dutch East India Company governor general in 1609, the administration of justice was handled by the first admiral to arrive at a given destination.

The admiral and his council of ship's officers were responsible for law and order both on sea and on land.[20] Through the admiral, the ship's laws were adapted to circumstances on land at the Dutch fortifications.

Dutch trading interests entangled the VOC increasingly in political relationships with the Company's established Southeast Asian counterparts, enhancing the need for an Asian-based polity that could negotiate treaties and conduct interstate diplomacy. From their earliest contact with Southeast Asia, the Dutch were aware that they were one among many powers in the region. Sultanates in Aceh, Banten, Ternate, and Makassar, for example, dominated extensive sea-based trading states that could not simply be overthrown as the Spanish had conquered the Aztecs. There was no real military or technological gap separating Southeast Asia from Europe that could not be quickly overcome. Coupled with European mortality, the presence of well-entrenched polities necessitated a diplomatic, internationalist approach to trade. According to Anthony Reid, "as the seventeenth century increased the level of commerce but reduced the number of diplomatic players [in Southeast Asia] to a few stronger states, these all established relations with one another."[21] Women played a crucial role in this new diplomacy. As the political stakes increased among the Southeast Asian powers, international alliances based on interstate marriages were crucial in cementing those alliances and preserving the delicate balance of regional power.

Many Southeast Asian kingdoms, especially the coastal Islamic states, were maritime trade empires like the Dutch.[22] When the Dutch arrived at their first port of call in Java (Banten) in 1596, they were met by the *shahbandar* (harbormaster) and assigned to a dock and trading stall next to the already established Portuguese, Gujaratis, Arabs, Chinese, and Bugis.[23] Savvy traders demanded Bengal cloth for spices and used Spanish and Japanese silver as currency.

This well-integrated system of international trade forced Dutch traders to establish a governmental apparatus in Asia that could act as a polity equivalent with other powers in the region. In other words Dutch economic interests required the promulgation of political structures and the legal codes that undergirded them. In turn, territorial administration required a "greater coordination of policy" and a more comprehensive legal code.[24] Given the eighteen- to twenty-four-month turnaround for a message to get to and from the East Indies, a separate ruling body—the Raad van Indië (Council of the Indies)—was set up in the Indies to govern Company affairs in Asia. By 1617 the duties of the governor general and his Council of the Indies were more clearly defined. The Raad charged one of its permanent members, the Advocaat-Fiskaal, with responsibility over legal and police matters.

The burdens and shortcomings of Dutch territorial administration were further intensified in 1619 by the acquisition of Jakarta (Batavia) on Java. Laws meant to apply to an all-male crew on the high seas proved grossly inadequate when dealing with questions of relations between different cultures and sexes. In the native-run ports, there had at least been a local legal framework forged from the combination of local *adat* (custom), Indian court canon (for example, the Manu Smriti or Laws of Manu), and Islamic law, which standardized weights and measures, regulated commerce, and redressed grievances. The Dutch were forced to ensure similar services at their port settlements in order to attract trade.

The first years of the Dutch East India Company's existence were marked by a steady transfer of sovereignty from the States General of the United Netherlands to the governor general at Batavia. Under the VOC charter, the Company was empowered to make treaties with "princes and potentates," erect fortifications, and administer justice in the East Indies in the name of the States General of the United Netherlands.[25] At the head of the Indies Hoge Regering in Asia was the governor general in Batavia. Alongside him was the Council of the Indies, with nine members—four members to oversee trade, the fleet, the military, and justice, respectively, and five members to direct the Company posts outside Batavia. While the officers of the Company and the Company itself were theoretically beholden to the States General for the renewal of their charter, the process of renewal became a mere formality. The States General's real influence in Company affairs came to a standstill when it ceased approving the official Company instructions in 1617 and appointed its last governor general in 1632. Distance hamstrung the Gentlemen in their ability to rule over Batavia in a meaningful way.

Article 8 of the instructions to the VOC's first governor general, drafted by the Gentlemen XVII and ratified by the States General in 1609, provides a window into the distance and difficulty involved in controlling what went on in a place referred to as "beyond the line" (which included the world to the east of the Cape of Good Hope). After explaining their model for the Indies government, the Gentlemen XVII were also forced to admit the virtual autonomy under which the governor general functioned: "Concerning how you [the governor general] shall conduct yourself in all other matters, the government, commerce, traffic, in addition to the alliances with the kings and potentates of the Indies, thereupon we can give you no fixed orders."[26] The last set of official instructions from the Gentlemen XVII to a governor general were made in 1650, and the Gentlemen XVII only rubber-stamped appointments (including that of a governor general) and statutes determined by the Hoge Regering.

In actual practice, the long arm of the law could not bridge the distance between the Netherlands and Asia; this would have to wait for the Suez Canal, steamships, and telegraph cable. Until then, the colonies handled legal matters on their own. Always functioning in the realm of the unprecedented, VOC law initially looked back to the United Provinces for guidance, but unfortunately the federal system in the Netherlands presented jurists with a different legal code for each province. So exactly *which* Dutch laws should be followed in Asia became a problem.

In a strange way, the Company's concern with the bottom line forced their legal structure to be less preoccupied with matters of race. Rather than legal privilege being tied to race, the primary distinction with regard to the administration of justice was Company employment. Legal scholar J. la Bree does not find that the colonial regime divided up its subjects along color lines. Instead the law separates Company personnel and their wives and slaves, on the one hand, and "European colonists, free indigenous, foreign Orientals, and slaves" on the other.[27]

In part, the English played an unwitting role in the construction of this system. Their ships, by the end of the sixteenth century, were plying Asian waters, and they emerged as fierce rivals to the Dutch. In Europe during the seventeenth and eighteenth centuries, the English fought four wars with the Dutch over commerce. Batavia's founder and the most influential man in the seventeenth-century VOC, Jan Pietersz Coen, called the English "arrogant competitors" and only reluctantly allowed them to establish a trade office at Batavia. Even after this concession, Coen denied them extraterritoriality and demanded that the English be subject to Dutch law. Within a year of

Batavia's founding in 1619, an incident helped persuade Coen to set VOC personnel apart from non-VOC as a way of targeting English competitors. Members of the English trade office in Batavia had taken it upon themselves to arrest a Chinese man and take him to their headquarters. Once inside, the Chinese man injured an Englishman, and the VOC decided to intervene. No authority was above that of the governor general, said Coen, and he seized the opportunity by arresting the injured Englishman and giving him a lashing. "To prevent other such instances," the High Government appointed Jan Steyns van Antwerpen as bailiff (*Baljuw*) on 29 March 1620. The appointment of a bailiff or city prosecutor in Batavia was one of the first sovereign acts performed by the VOC on Batavian soil, and the duties and instructions assigned to the bailiff further demonstrate the Dutch desire for this official to act as a check on English power. In addition to the protection of Dutch conquests and trade, the bailiff was charged with "building a good city" and "maintaining the sovereignty of the land against the penetration of the English."[28] Months after the incident with the Chinese man and the Englishman, the VOC established the Court of Aldermen to pursue the legal process against non-VOC residents of Batavia, and by 1625 there were two autonomous city prosecutors, the fiscal advocate and the bailiff, each running his own police force and presenting cases to the respective Company and municipal courts.[29]

VOC officials were willing to do whatever it took to squeeze the English out of the market. The VOC accorded Company wives the status of their husbands. Even slaves of Company personnel appeared before the Council of Justice, while European and Asian free burghers, even though hired out by the Company, did not appear before that VOC court but, instead, before the municipal Court of Aldermen. La Bree sees the Company/non-Company dichotomy as the closest the law came to codifying the population. "This distinction into groups," notes La Bree, "is the primary guide for arriving at an approximate [legal] definition."[30]

On one side of this legal divide, the Schepenbank, if not the "privileged forum" that was the Council of Justice, was a fascinating institution within the VOC machinery. The Schepenbank originated in the Netherlands. In the early modern Dutch Republic, cities formed the source of power and authority. Although part of a province in a Republic, municipalities essentially administered themselves. Medieval drainage boards—having evolved as a practical necessity to keep the region from being constantly inundated with water—appeared as the first governing bodies in the Low Countries. Increasing mercantile prosperity and urbanization throughout the late medieval and early modern period produced equally pragmatic civic institutions as merchant elites came to dominate society.[31] In most cities, prominent plutocrats were chosen to form a court of aldermen. For example, an early modern observer described Leiden as having been ruled by the aldermen and under the count of Holland "since antiquity."[32]

The Company brought this Dutch legal institution to the Indies in order to provide justice for the non-VOC community. Generally, the Court of Aldermen consisted of a mix of nine of the "most skilled officers of the fort in the service of the VOC," among "the most distinguished, capable and honest of the leading burgers of this city," and "one of the most distinguished of the [Chinese] nation."[33] The High Government appointed aldermen for one-year terms that could be renewed indefinitely. For their services, the government gave the aldermen fixed salaries, a share of the fines levied, a special seat in church services, and an exemption from sumptuary laws forbidding the wearing of excessive gold and silver jewelry. Although the aldermen supervised various duties of civic administration, including overseeing estate sales, censuses, and weights and measures, their primary task involved sitting in judgment of cases brought before them by the city prosecutor.

Batavia's founders recognized the need for and implemented separate Company and municipal court systems. The Indies government armed the bailiff, working under the municipal courts, with his own police force, which he paid and outfitted from the fines he collected. In a 1622 colonial statute we read that the bailiff was given command over "4 strapping Germans and four black officers," who were referred to as *kaffirs*.[34] The kaffirs came allegedly from East Africa and wore red. Later eighteenth-century court proceedings still referred to the policemen as kaffirs, but they were more likely of Madurese origin. With his kaffirs, the bailiff remained in close communication with the neighborhood leaders (*wijkmeesteren*) and with the heads of the various ethnic communities (*hoofden*) both inside and outside the city. In the city proper, the bailiff and the kaffirs could make the necessary arrests and conduct a criminal investigation when a crime was committed. But, as we shall see, private individuals conducted their own investigations and delivered crucial evidence and suspects to the Schepenbank. However collected, after the bailiff gathered evidence and statements, he then presented the case to the Court of Aldermen.

Of utmost importance, the Raad van Justitie (or Justitie) was much better equipped than the Court of Aldermen to try complicated questions of inheritance and complex civil and criminal proceedings. Although still under the governor general, the Justitie was staffed by important Chinese and European civilians who were not necessarily legal professionals. The staff served double duty by running the local police force alongside the aldermen's deputies.[35] Early instructions to the Justitie required it be staffed with trained jurists.[36] Many in the Schepenbank received their training on the ground in Batavia. Compared to the relatively small percentage of Batavia's population who fell under the jurisdiction of the Justitie, the masses inside and outside Batavia were subject to an overworked Schepenbank. It did function, but the Schepenbank remained, in many ways, a court inferior to the Justitie.

Extractions from criminal proceedings in the Schepenbank give a sense of how the court functioned. Investigations lacked checks and balances, and the Schepenbank's pretrial criminal process could be arbitrary and personality driven. One day in 1793, for instance, a Chinese woman named Nioknio discovered an intruder in her home. The intruder, a man named Madie, was attempting to steal the candelabra that Nioknio kept on an offering table in her entryway.[37] With the candelabra bundled in his sarong, Madie fled to the river and there deposited his contraband. Nioknio and her husband, Lim Joepet, called for the bailiff, and along with a kaffir they apprehended Madie and retrieved the candelabra. Several days later the *Landdrost* bailiff, Steven Poelman, ordered all involved to appear before the Schepenbank as he prosecuted the case against Madie. So it often occurred that the bailiff conducted the criminal investigation, acted as law enforcement, and prosecuted the case before the Schepenbank.

As Batavia began expanding, the bailiff was unable to cover the expanses outside the city walls, and so another prosecutor was appointed, known as a *Landdrost*, to be responsible for Batavia's environs. The landdrost (also known as the Drossaart or *Drost*) was essentially a second bailiff, and his title came from the officer who oversaw justice in the Dutch countryside with the assistance of Asian notables. For example, one night near Bandung, a fight broke out over who would get to dance with the performing *ronggeng* girls, and a

Javanese stableman named Soeta stabbed his fellow stableman, Landjiep, dead with a *kris* (Malay dagger). Soeta was apprehended and brought before the regional headman, the *Tommongong Angadiridja* of Bandung, who promptly turned him over to the landdrost. Court records show a Javanese letter from Tommongong Angadiridja stating that "Soeta van Tjikow has confessed to me that he had gone amok at the *ronggeng* and killed another man."[38] Thus, especially in areas outside Batavia's city walls, the Schepenbank employed a network of Asian community leaders to help with its administration of justice, though these environs were under direct municipal control.

The criminal trial itself was governed by its own set of rules and procedures. When a crime had been committed and a suspect apprehended, the bailiff would prepare an indictment (*versoek*) against the accused and present it to the Schepenbank, often the next day. The indictment briefly stated the crime that was charged and sought the court's permission to conduct the necessary depositions (*declaratoiren*) and interrogations. Usually within a week of the indictment, witnesses and defendants were brought in to testify before the bailiff, several members of the Schepenbank, and the clerks and translators. If the defendant confessed, the interrogation was called as such (*confessie*), and the court proceeded to sentencing. In the case of a denial, the court had other means at its disposal.

A confession was important to the Schepenbank. According to Roman Dutch law, in the absence of a confession, noncircumstantial evidence and multiple eyewitnesses (normally three) were required to sentence someone to death. Civil proceedings required only single eyewitness accounts and circumstantial evidence. The criminal code was more demanding. The aforementioned Soeta did not initially confess to the murder, and Tommongong Angadiridja's testimony notwithstanding, the prosecutor sought and received permission to conduct a "sharp examination" to extract the confession (*eijsch ad torturam*) necessary to put him to death.[39]

Failing a confession, the aldermen were unable to deliver capital punishment. When a recently freed slave, Damon van Batavia, was accused of murdering the new love interest of Damon's former lover, the slavin Tjoelan van Makasar, he refused to confess and could only be fined with court costs and be banned from the city.[40] The Schepenbank had to conclude that "the inconsistency of the indictment, the lack of evidence, and the necessity of his confession" were "all points that make it necessary to exercise more latitude."[41]

Another method for the Schepenbank to get information and verify testimony was the *recolement*. This entailed the process of reading previous statements of defendants and witnesses back to them and asking them to attest to their truthfulness and if necessary to amend their contents. Normally seven days after the initial statement, the individual would be brought back to court for the recolement, which often (but not always) amounted to a routine affirmation of the initial statement. The recolement was also a chance for the individual to sign his or her name or leave a mark, and to take (or not, in the case of slaves) a ritual oath according to one's cultural and/or religious conventions.

Adriana Philadelphia Thomas, born in Batavia, was a free Christian woman and the "*nonje* or housekeeper" of an innkeeper named Jan Smit, who—along with Thomas Williams (Adriana's godfather) and three Chinese named Tio Tjoeko, Lim Tingko, and Ong Tsjioeko—was on trial for smuggling eighty-three balls of opium. Laying her hand on the Dutch Reformed *Staten Bijbel*, Adriana swore that she minded her own business at the inn and did not witness any illegal activity, though she "had a feeling" that the accused must be dealing opium when the men would arrive with "sap" that they claimed came from Smit's seashore garden.[42]

In another case, a Chinese pig butcher called Lim Kinko swore an oath "in the Chinese fashion."[43] He said he returned home one evening from the market and found his slavin/concubine/wife Balij van Balij and his concubine/wife Nio Kinnio on the floor in a pool of blood after trading hatchet blows in a bout of jealousy.[44] At the same trial, two neighbor women (presumably *peranakan*) named Imnio and Si Balij reported hearing Lim's "Chinese wife" Nio Kinnio call for help. Both Imnio and Si Balij swore an oath "according to the Mohammedan custom" by "the laying of the first two fingers of the right hand on al-Koran."[45]

Anyone could testify before the Court of Aldermen, but special provisions were made in the case of slaves and others, including the elderly.[46] Slaves delivered testimony just like any other witness or defendant and signed their names or left a mark at the recolement, but they swore no oath. This practice was repeated throughout the criminal proceedings, and definitive proof that slaves swore no legal oath is found in the case of the "enterprising" runaway slavin Sitie van Makasar. In one *declaratoir*, six people gave essentially the same statement (Mochamat Tsikini, a Moor; Pier Mochaman, also a Moor; Bappa Salee, a peranakan Chinese; Oeij Loanko, a Chinese man; Na Kienseeng, a Chinese woman; and Jamia, a slavin). All but the slavin, Jamia, took an oath.[47] However, aside from this procedural difference, slave testimony seems to have been given the same weight as any other evidence at trial.

On occasion, an individual decided to change or amend his or her statement. Then, the recolement became anything but a reiteration, as changes in testimony ran the gamut from subtle nuancing to dramatic reversal. On 17 December 1790, when a Chinese woman, Lim Siongnio, saw that her husband's chances for an acquittal in his nutmeg smuggling case were dwindling and that the prosecution had requested permission to use torture during his interrogation, she decided to alter her statement.[48] Previously, she swore that her husband, Njio Tiongko, had told her that an unnamed Chinese man had accidentally left a bag of nutmeg at their house while Njio was busy weighing cloves. Njio opened it, saw that it was nutmeg, and ran after the Chinese man to give it back to him, when he ran into some officials who confiscated the nutmeg. A week later at her recolement, Lim was telling a slightly different story. She had been mistaken, she said. Her husband had not told her about the abandoned nutmeg, but she herself had witnessed the unnamed Chinese leave it behind.[49]

Tjoelan van Makasar (the slavin involved in the love triangle) revised her 11 August 1789 statement not once, but a rare two times. In the first instance, she was forced to explain why two fellow slavinnen, Sara van Amboina and Aspasia van Boegis, both gave testimony that contradicted hers. Tjoelan had stated that by the time of the murder she had already crossed the street with her mistress, Juffrouw Arnolda Daniels (Daniels was a widow to a man named Vos), and entered the house of their friend, the Widow Lugthard. Sara and Aspasia both maintained that, while Tjoelan had indeed gone to the Widow Lugthard's, she had returned to the home of Juff. Daniels and was busy sewing when the cry of amok rang out.[50] On 27 August, Tjoelan modified her initial statement by admitting that she had been home at the time of the murder but insisted she still did not know how the slave Maas van Batavia had become wounded.[51] Perhaps she knew the Roman Dutch law and how difficult it would be to convict

Damon without eyewitness testimony and without his confession. Later, in an extremely rare second modification to her statement, Tjoelan said that, while Maas and Damon were sitting on her mistress's front step, she heard Maas say that "his heart could not rest until he could give Damon a beating."[52] Aspasia also later changed her testimony, saying that as soon as they heard the commotion in front of the door, they locked it. They admitted seeing Maas and Damon wrestling with each other from the window. And so, to try and pin down the slippery truths in cases such as Damon's, the Court of Aldermen employed other techniques.

One of the most fascinating and dramatic conventions of Schepenbank information gathering was known as the "points of confrontation." In instances where many versions and reversions of events muddied the legal waters, the court sat the conflicting witnesses down together and had them square off in a contest for the truth. On 27 August 1789, Damon, Tjoelan, Sara, Aspasia, and Avontuur van Sumbauwa (the slave who restrained Damon) were made to debate the points of confrontation in their testimonies. The Schepenbank was trying to nail down a timeline for Maas's murder and to cross-check stories and alibis.

The points of confrontation could become particularly heated (and informative) when the legal inquiry turned into a "he-said she-said" interchange between estranged lovers. Lewat van Timor was in an intimate relationship with Pama van Bugis, much to the dismay of Pama's mother, Indock van Bugis. All were slaves of the Chinese Gouw Koko, and when Koko refused to get involved in the affairs of Indock's daughter, Indock became more confrontational toward Lewat, until one morning the mother was found wrapped tightly in a mat, face down in a mud pool on a Chinese plantation, with her throat slit. Lewat went missing, and four months later he was picked up in Banten and brought to face not only the aldermen but also other witnesses with whom Lewat's testimony conflicted. When asked if the couple had Indock's blessing, Lewat answered an emphatic "Yes!" but Pama said "No!" adding that Lewat fought daily with her mother. According to Lewat, Pama had begged him to spirit her away from Koko, but Pama shot back with the reply, "That is not true. That night he asked me to get him out." Four Balinese fellow slavinnen, one Balinese slave, and Master Koko all took turns with Pama, facing Lewat and refuting his story. The intensity of the confrontation often delivered the aldermen results and, as in the case of Lewat and the others, the coveted confession.

The Schepenbank enforced the separation of the population into VOC and non-VOC. This divide was the most fundamental and important legal distinction in the early modern Dutch colonies and was done away with in the nineteenth century when demographic and economic conditions changed. Dutch decision-makers exercised steely pragmatism in the architecture of their legal system, and its legitimacy was grounded in deeper structural truths. Demographic, economic, and political economic factors shaped the decision to promulgate a law code that privileged a new female elite while enshrining an increasingly permanent new underclass.

The practical considerations of the need for marriage partners for Company men and the desire for an exclusive and exclusionary court system for the families of those partnerships governed VOC law and practice. Indeed, pragmatism in the pursuit of profits was at the heart of VOC activity. The results were sometimes shockingly brutal, but the lust for lucre also led the VOC down what were by contemporary standards some surprisingly enlightened and progressive avenues. The Dutch were able to cohabit and intermarry with the Asian community simply because racial mixing was more practical and realistic— practically no European women made the voyage to Asia, and in some cases tolerance paid off.

When tolerance paid, the VOC practiced it, and when it did not Company prejudice was extreme. If it was necessary to marry local women in order to create a network within a local economy, or if it was necessary to exterminate the urban Chinese in order to preserve Company hegemony, then the Company had no misgivings doing either. If the Company could monopolize the delivery of trade goods through friendly alliances with sultanates and princedoms, then so be it, but an island that refused to cooperate could well be razed and its inhabitants slaughtered.[53] With a fiscal compass as its primary navigational tool, the world's first joint stock company made decisions, including legal decisions, calculated to enhance its profitability. Pragmatism is the most important explanatory key to VOC colonial behavior.

Batavia and

Its Runaway Slavinnen

One day in the early months of 1793, authorities became suspicious when they noticed a man carrying what appeared to be a bloody axe (in Malay, *gollok*). When they approached him about the axe (which turned out only to have rust on the blade), they discovered that he was in fact a fugitive slave. The runaway, named Augusto van Sumbauwa, revealed to them a complex of safe houses and runaway accomplices. Augusto had been on the run with his girlfriend, Sapia van Sumbauwa, moving from safe house to safe house. They had first rented a back room in the house of a "free non-Christian woman" called Ma (or Nyai) Sauwa, partially in exchange for repairing her roof.[1] Then they moved to a large plantation mansion with other runaways. The mansion belonged to the captain of the Moors, Mochamat Alie, and one of the foremen (*mandor*) on his sprawling estate, Djemal, was using the mansion to house fugitive slaves, primarily couples.[2]

Sapia and several of her slavin friends had chosen to run away from their owners. They had done so when denied the opportunity to move ahead in life and start a family each with their would-be spouse. For example, one of the slavinnen, Serana van Batavia (alias Ma Abas) ran away "for no good reason," according to her master, the Moor Dauod Aboe Bakar. However, Serana did have reasons. She fled in order to have a child with her new boyfriend after her master sold her former husband.[3]

As these examples suggest, the slavinnen and their masters represented competing notions of slavery and dependence in Batavia. As long as slavery has existed, so too have fugitive slaves, and the reasons behind both phenomena are as varied as the nature of human bondage itself. In Batavia, some ran away because of physically abusive mistresses, while others fled less blatant torments. Forms of slavery and human bondage existed in Southeast Asia long before and long after the arrival of the Europeans in the archipelago. Whereas a Western presence in Africa and the Americas set in motion new modes of slavery and introduced unprecedented numbers of people to the practice, the early modern European presence in Asia had neither of these effects but, instead, fed off an existing slave trade, with the newcomers cornering slave markets much as they did the clove markets. The age of commerce in Southeast Asia—commerce in both humans and fine spices—predated the joint stock companies, but with the coming (and, most important, with the record keeping) of the VOC, not only are we able to keep a head count of slave traffic and population in the colony, we are also given access to the courtroom dramas giving narrative content to a population that was previously nameless and faceless. Equally important, the slave narratives taken in criminal proceedings also provide windows into the slowly changing relationship between Europe and Asia in the early modern era.

Crimes of every sort and severity could land one of Batavia's lesser individuals in jail and on trial. In Batavia's Court of Aldermen, slaves and slavinnen stood alongside non-slaves accused of many of the same crimes—but the statutes reserved one offense in particular for them, running away (*weglopen*). Here we'll be looking at the criminal cases dealing with Batavian slavinnen who ran away from their masters and mistresses and were obviously unsuccessful, because they were captured and had to stand trial.

Why did they run? Part of the answer, I argue, has to do with the colonial capital itself. First, Roman Dutch law compromised an important pillar of the Southeast Asian society—social mobility. On the one hand, this may seem contradictory given that many Asian women used the law, through marriage and remarriage, to ascend to the ranks of Batavia's elite. However, for underclass women outside the Company, Batavia's Roman Dutch statutes set up a firm partition between free and slave. The codification of slave versus free substituted a rigid dichotomy for fluid abstract conceptions of social hierarchy, in effect clogging up the flow of underclass mobility.[4] In addition, the growing plantation economy around Batavia, presaging things to come throughout the archipelago, eroded the previous filial relationship between mistress and slavin into a mere money relationship. So Batavia itself helped to create the phenomenon of the runaway slavin. Second, if the colonial capital created conditions for slavinnen to want to run away, it also provided opportunities for them to do so. The relative anonymity of the city and its extensive underclass community opened up avenues and connections for flight, even as it left slavinnen on the run vulnerable to deception, abduction, and abuse.

SOUTHEAST ASIAN SOCIAL SYSTEMS

Scholars have often described the status of individuals within Southeast Asian social systems as historically interdependent and mobile, and here the question of slavery is of particular importance.[5] Rather than finding themselves in a strict and permanent categorization of human beings as either independent free individuals or enslaved subjects, Southeast Asians typically found themselves both acting as patrons, with their own network of clients, and at the same time serving in relationships of dependence toward others. Slaves and slavinnen purchased at auction, for example, themselves could command bondservants partially beholden to them.[6] Rather than freedom forming one side of an either/or dichotomy opposed to slavery, in Southeast Asia freedom and slavery were more accurately defined as abstract and opposite ends of a sliding social continuum. To further complicate matters, "freedom" was situational and not something necessarily reducible to a final sum on a balance sheet. At certain times of the year, an individual might be subject to onerous, even slave labor while in other contexts he or she might enjoy a remarkable degree of autonomy. This high level of social interdependence was rooted largely in geographic realities that also influenced the shape of political systems in Southeast Asia.

As Reid (among others) has pointed out, "the key to Southeast Asian social systems was the control of men," not land.[7] Relatively low population density throughout the region conspired with an extremely mobile populace, especially in the archipelago, to create a pattern of reciprocal rule. People sought the protection and prosperity afforded by a given ruler's circle of influence (*mandala*), and that ruler's power and prestige expanded as more and more people attached themselves to the realm. Moreover, peasants were not perpetually tied to the land as were their contemporaries in Europe. In Southeast Asia, should a ruler's yoke become too onerous, the lure of a neighboring kingdom, easy seaborne transport, low population density, and cheap and abundant building materials allowed families and populations the opportunity to move and seek their fortunes elsewhere. In Southeast Asia "power" was "manpower," and nowhere is this idea more clearly demonstrated than in the nature of warfare among rival kingdoms. Contests were seldom about conquering territory but were frequently about capturing rival armies and populations. So as not to damage the prized human capital, battles were often symbolic and relatively little blood would be spilled on the field. Captured armies and peoples were taken by the victors, quickly assimilated by the conquerors, and eventually allowed social mobility.[8]

Furthermore, borders between principalities and sultanates were porous or nonexistent. As Benedict Anderson described the situation on Java: "kingdoms were not regarded as having fixed and charted limits, but rather flexible, fluctuating perimeters. In a real sense, there were no political frontiers at all, the Power of one ruler gradually fading into the distance and merging imperceptibly with the ascending Power of a neighboring sovereign."[9] More than any other factor, the possibility of mobility held a sovereign's power in check. On a societal level, this potential mobility functioned in much the same way that the threat of divorce did in Southeast Asian marriages. Knowing that women had extramarital social and economic opportunities forced men to share power in the relationship and to work for their spouses' affection. Southeast Asian sovereigns knew that their "subjects" also had options outside the realm, and this had a mitigating effect on any royal aspirations to absolute authority, giving people power to vote with their feet. But just because people could relocate did not mean they necessarily exercised the privilege. For an underling, a simple appraisal of costs and benefits might show that the dangers of the unknown outweighed the benefits of relocation. Defaulting on a perceived social obligation was undoubtedly a major decision and one not to be taken lightly. The point is that the potential for flight and social mobility, the dependence of clients on their patrons, and most important the reliance of patrons on their clients modified the way people interacted with each other to such an extent that one's circumstances seldom came to flight.[10]

This negotiated relationship between sovereign and subject was replicated all along the social scale from the ruling class down to the underclass. Swidden farmers taken in a slave raid or soldiers captured in warfare might find themselves incorporated into some household's domestic service or into the wet rice agricultural complex, or adopted directly into a family. In order to bury a parent, raise a bride price, or pay a gambling debt, people would also willingly incur debt bondage or enter into concubinage (we find a particularly stunning example of this among our court cases, the case of Nio Kinnio in Chapter 3). Rather than suffering permanent juridical slave status, they could move within the social hierarchy as they intermarried, worked off their debt, and took on clients of their own. As the historian Michael Aung Thwin has stated, "the important question was to whom you were bonded rather than the abstract legal quality of your bondage."[11] In turn, their masters would probably be financially and socially beholden to others, and so these "stratified clusters of patron-client relationships" continued on up to the sovereign.[12]

Southeast Asia's cultural matrix was not only complex and its society interconnected, but it was also extremely open and adept at assimilating outsiders and their ideas, which allowed for a high degree of individual social mobility. For centuries Southeast Asia (and especially Indonesia) has been a crossroads for traffic in commerce and ideas. Java's massive, millennium-old Hindu and Buddhist monuments testify to the region's ancient connection with the Indian Ocean world, just as Java's *wayang* tells of the Indonesianization of those traditions and their epics. Onion-domed mosques and cross-shaped cathedrals tell of more recent encounters with ideologies from beyond the archipelago and of the incorporation of these worldviews into Indonesia's cultural fabric.

Commercial traffic has been just as brisk—and probably ultimately responsible for or at least the bearer of—the traffic in intellectual and spiritual property. Already in the fifteenth century, the Indonesian archipelago stood at the center of a great international trading network connecting India and the Middle East to China through Southeast Asia, with Europe receiving small but valuable quantities of the Asian goods. Each year by the thousands, foreign merchants would sail the monsoon winds to, from, and through maritime Southeast Asia, selling their various cargoes of rice, salt, aromatic woods, precious stones and metals, furs and silks and other textiles, porcelain, pepper, and fine spices to other traders gathered there, buying their goods in return. Powerful early modern Malay trading states with urban populations of one or two hundred thousand such as Melaka on the Malay peninsula and Makassar in South Sulawesi attracted Arab, Indian, Chinese, and Southeast Asian merchants by providing essentially free-market ports, warehouse facilities, an adequate legal system, and by policing the waterways for pirates. State and local interdependence within the region combined with trade and traffic from outside the region to allow for great social mobility in Southeast Asia. Society did not fix status and rank at birth; they were always subject to a person's fortunes in the market of mutual obligation and in the making and breaking of patron-client relationships.

Historian Oliver Wolters has cited individual charisma as an important feature of the Southeast Asian "cultural matrix."[13] His notion of the "man of prowess" is a critical component in the self-made nature of pre- and early modern status in the region. People chose to follow a given leader based not solely on his or her lineage but more on the self-made qualities of prowess, pluck, and prescience. On a popular level, bilateral or cognatic kinship was one manifestation of how the man or woman of prowess could play out in Southeast Asian kinship structures. Rather than inheritance or dominion being passed automatically through the eldest son (primogeniture), it passed to the most "worthy" child, male or female, or it could also be divided among all the siblings. Bravery in battle, grace under pressure, rhetorical skill, and financial acumen were all characteristics with which individuals could distinguish themselves, thus increasing the odds of attracting important patrons, clients, and social ties.

CIVIL LAW AND THE COLONIAL CAPITAL

The traditional practices and implicit understandings of debt bondage and obligation were insufficient for some foreign merchants, not only the Dutch, who needed statutory legal assurances that the slaves whom they viewed as their property would behave as such.[14] Batavia's cosmopolitan populace, hailing from every corner of the world, did not share an unspecified set of cultural assumptions among them; some commercial assumptions, however, were mutual and held dear. Reid and others have pointed to the lack of safeguards for private property, with the requisite legal and governmental apparatus to support it, as a crucial factor marking Southeast Asia's early modern divergence from the West. In the areas under its control, the VOC labored to establish a place where financial institutions and markets could flourish and where merchants would not hesitate to accumulate and develop fixed capital. Ultimately the fluidity and easy flight inherent in the Southeast Asian social system proved too dangerous for the Company's fixed and hard commercial interests. Roman Dutch law provided those firm boundaries and clear distinctions; it also left an otherwise mobile slave underclass with few choices but to run away. Batavian statutory law collapsed this complicated network of Southeast Asian vertical bonding into the simple dichotomy of slave versus free, concretized what had been fluid, temporary social arrangements, and closed off avenues for social mobility.

The nature of the colonial legal system itself, in addition to the substantive content of its statutes, was antithetical to social innovation. Colonial Roman Dutch law was a civil law code, as opposed to common law as practiced in Britain and elsewhere, and the distinction is important.[15] In a civil law tradition, judges viewed the law code as a comprehensive body of rules and regulations, always referring the facts in a given case back against that original corpus. Juries and defense attorneys, for example, were deemed unnecessary because justice in the form of the court, far from being blind, looked directly at the accused and decided if and to what extent they stood in violation of the statutes. Rather than providing a more neutral common law venue in which prosecution and defense square off before a jury to decide the merits of a case, the civil law judiciary functioned as prosecution and defense, judge and jury. Furthermore, the judicial system did not ask civil law judges to interpret the law or to break new legal ground in their rulings. Innovation was the job of legislators who created and amended the law code. In civil law, therefore, case law and legal precedence had no bearing. As such, civil law was much less flexible and adaptable to changing custom or circumstance. Rather than the common law practice of constant reinterpretation and refashioning of the law, case by case and hence moment to moment, civil law decisions referred back to the code. Only legislative overhaul of the existing code or promulgation of a new code could update the law to reflect shifting mores and values.

Civil law codification of slavery reduced traditional Southeast Asian forms of slavery, bondage, and dependency to something approaching chattel bondage. A prominent—some would say essential—part of the region's cultural matrix was the ability to adapt to change and to incorporate exogenous elements while maintaining indigenous integrity.[16] Laws, local and colonial, were and are traditional recipes of a social soup that was constantly evolving. Statutory law in particular did violence to a society in which change and constant flux were essential. Instead, the statutes of Batavia imposed European conceptions of lifelong bondage. Although the statutes themselves were a negotiation between Roman Dutch law and the economic needs and demographic exigencies of Dutch colonialism, they were unresponsive to traditional Asian social practice on the ground. The "cultural assumptions that debt entailed obligation were insufficient" in Batavia's cosmopolitan context.[17] Moreover, merchants expected the VOC to protect their belongings, and the Council of the Indies specifically designed the laws to ensure that their slaves remained slaves, property remained property.

The VOC helped create runaway slavinnen by creating a reason for dependants to run away, namely, substituting a restrictive system of slavery for the previously fluid system of vertical bonding, but Batavia unintentionally provided the means for them to do so. The urban (in this case, the colonial capital) gave rise to a host of new paradoxes and contradictory possibilities for slavinnen looking to escape slavery. On the one hand, eighteenth-century Batavia saw the tightening of a juridically defined slavery that provided an impetus for flight, while on the other it offered the anonymity and networking necessary for escape. For a woman who could not have gone unnoticed and unaccounted for in a small village setting, the big city with its transient and teeming population provided the requisite anonymity for a slavin to slip away, pose as free, and blend into the sea of faces. Conversely, this urban vacuity and nameless isolation left underclass women vulnerable to abduction and abuse from predators lurking unnoticed on the margins of the horde, preying on the vulnerable and unseen; anonymity was perhaps the city's most important runaway resource and also its most dangerous. Batavia was far removed from a setting where everyone appreciated, and laws were unnecessary to convey, the fact that debt entailed obligation and where local ties held patrons and clients together. A city of immigrants, Batavia was also far removed from a community of certainties, securities, and protections.

RUNAWAYS—THE CASES

Danie

While walking near Batavia's Jassenbrug bridge one August morning in 1791, Jiemoen, a peranakan Chinese boy, noticed something just visible in the canal below. Upon closer inspection he discovered to his horror that it was the body of his "good friend" Tompel, whose submerged body bobbed beneath the surface of the water with a noose wrenched around her neck. Jiemoen informed authorities that Tompel, a twelve-year-old girl, was the slavin of the Chinese woman Gouw Bianio, but no one seemed to know how she had ended up strangled and "left prey to the current of the water." Muddying the already murky details surrounding the girl's death, Tompel's mistress also discovered that her own jewelry box, containing the enormous sum of thirteen hundred rijksdaalders in diamond and gold jewelry, was missing.[18] Landdrost Steven Poelman painted the picture of the uncertainty that prevailed over the case, "The circumstances of Tompel's terrible death were a mystery. There was suspicion of seduction [that is, kidnapping] yet who had murdered her remained an unsolved puzzle. And where was the missing chest? No one, not the prosecutor . . . nor [Gouw Bianio] knew how Tompel was taken from her home and where she was killed. It seemed that this would forever remain a secret."[19]

Gouw Bianio's brother, Gouw Tjansie, was the powerful "Lieutenant of the Chinese nation" in Batavia and as such not only represented his people to the VOC authorities but also was able to marshal his considerable resources in solving the crime. As with most slave crimes, investigators closely scrutinized other slaves as potential conspirators. The combing by Tjansie and his *mata mata* (Malay, meaning literally "eyes," that is, spies) through Bianio's house staff, turned up no leads.[20] Everyone had rock-solid alibis, especially Tompel's fellow slavin, Danie van Sumbauwa, who had been with her mistress when the crime was committed. For several days there was no movement in the investigation and no clues other than the body and the missing jewelry. Then, suddenly, the case broke open when Danie van Sumbauwa came forward "of her own accord" and began talking, according to the Landdrost, "pained by the sting of her own conscience." The complicated story that Danie related reveals much more than the circumstances surrounding the death of a slave girl. It further chronicles the erosion of binding, even sentimental, family ties between slavin and mistress in the world of the nascent plantation economy. The dramatic turn of events in Tompel's murder highlight the drastic lengths that many were willing to go to in order to break the legal chain that kept them confined to the lowest rung of the social ladder.

The wealthy Chinese mistress, Gouw Bianio, was not Danie's first owner. Danie had served under previous mistresses. During one of these tours of duty, she made the acquaintance of an Amien van Bugis, who was the property of a neighboring master. Especially when the nature of the relationship between slavin and mistress was purely transactional and economic, the affinities of a slavin became oriented even more strongly toward fellow slaves with whom she already shared many of the same material circumstances of life. On August 25, 1791, while out on an errand for Bianio, Danie paid a visit to the market stall (in Malay, *warong*) of her old neighbor Amien. Danie was visibly sick, and as she sat eating pineapple by the warong one of Amien's visiting friends asked Danie about her mistress, saying "How could Nyai send you now, still being sick? Why don't you escape from her?" The questions came from a slave named Akier van Bali who himself belonged to a Chinese mistress, Nyai Lotje. Akier spent most of his days running others' wares back and forth to Tanah Abang in a *prauw* (a canoe-like boat; in Malay, *perahu*), "where," he said, "I earn a schelling each market day for my mistress," in addition to other days when he did "housework for my Nyai."[21] According to Danie, Akier offered to spirit her away in his perahu and encouraged her to make off with some of Gouw Bianio's property as well. Danie agreed.

Two days later at the market, Danie said, there was another meeting between her and Amien and Akier. They asked if she had been able to get hold of her mistress's valuables. This would be difficult, but Danie had a plan. She called Tompel over from a neighboring warong and introduced her to the others. From the testimonies, it appears that Tompel too was unhappy with her life. Akier quoted Danie as saying, "My little friend [Tompel] gets hit by her Nyai and wants to run away."[22] Court records paint Tompel as "her mistress's confidante." It was decided between Danie, Tompel, Amien, and Akier that the little girl would steal the valuables because, Danie said, Tompel "had the best opportunity to do so because she spent most of her time by and with the mistress."[23]

On a rainy Monday night, 29 August 1791, at 7 o'clock, Amien showed up in the canal behind Gouw Bianio's with Akier's boat. Inexplicably, Akier was not in the boat, but a fellow slave, Lepo van Bugis, instead accompanied Amien. According to Danie, Tompel had managed to sneak away with the jewelry box and they were heading for the boat when their mistress's voice suddenly rang out, calling for Danie. Frozen, Danie ordered Tompel to head for the perahu while she returned to Gouw Bianio. When Danie returned canal side a few minutes later, the perahu was gone. Literally and figuratively, she had missed the boat. "Fear," said Danie, made her keep her secret, but after five days, compelled by her conscience, she began telling her story and naming accomplices, who each then presented his or her own story.

While conflicting accounts may leave the circumstances of Tompel's murder in question, they do clarify the social situation for much of Batavia's late eighteenth-century slave population. The law may have bound slaves to their masters, but their affinities proved difficult to legislate. Instead of owners adopting slaves into their permanent family network, slaves were market commodities who changed hands frequently and failed to develop bonds of trust and affinity with their owners. Instead, slaves nurtured their own, often horizontal, networks of contacts and confidants with fellow slaves and neighbors. Absent the reciprocal relationships in which slave devotion brought filial promotion and freedom, running away seemed the only avenue for upward advancement.

Thanks to the Chinese lieutenant and the persistent questioning of the aldermen, we are offered a glimpse of the network employed by Danie and others involved in their scheme. Gouw Tjansie not only broke the case, getting Danie to testify, but he seems also to have conducted most of the arrests and initial interrogations before turning the defendants over to the Schepenen. Danie led investigators to Amien and Akier, who told Tjansie that they had simply come across Tompel's body and the jewelry in the water. Akier acknowledged that his boat may have been involved in the crime, but he was not. He told of how Danie approached him about helping her and Tompel run away, but, he said, "I turned her down directly . . . [because] I must stay with my poor, broke Nyai."[24] Amien van Bugis and Lepo van Bugis were in dispute over who had actually committed the murder. Lepo said that Amien had put the rope around Tompel's neck and that he had merely helped restrain her. Amien said they (including Danie) had planned to kill the girl, but that Lepo alone began strangling her with the noose.[25] Amien too informed on a friend, Mingo van Bali, with whom he had been a fellow slave under a Chinese rice-wine distiller.[26] Mingo and his brother Laijseeng van Bali had acted as fences for the stolen goods and had sent the stolen pieces out to be melted down or radically altered so that they would be unrecognizable.[27]

An interconnected web of friends, neighbors, and former fellow slaves knit this crime together, and its unraveling dragged all connected before the aldermen's bench. Punishments ranged from death for the murderers, to sentences of between fifteen and fifty years of hard labor for others involved. Danie's sentence was unique because she had neither actually stolen anything nor run away from her mistress. Instead, the court cited Danie as the "principle source" for the wrongs committed by all the others, because of her "silence in an unforgivable secret." Drossart Steven Poelman summarized the Court's position:

> With a simple word, Danie could have prevented everything and from whom the smallest token of loyalty would have been enough to save a person's life, would have had time to spare her mistress this great blow, might have saved from the vengeful hand of an uncompromising justice a few of her fellow beings who because of her behavior all underwent a villainous transformation, and finally would not have exposed herself to a danger by which she certainly would have been destroyed. This all seemed unimportant enough to her and she could only achieve her goal by following through with them to whom she gave herself willingly."[28]

The aldermen reasoned that while she could not be given capital punishment under the strict laws on domestic theft, she was guilty as the crime's catalyst. They charged Danie as an accessory to domestic theft and to the kidnapping, ordered her to view the public deaths of Amien and Lepo, and sent her to labor on the public works for fifty years.

Christina

If allowed to experience some degree of family intimacy as a real part of their owner's family or with their own spouses and children, many slaves were willing to tolerate their position. Some aspired to wealth, riches, and swift social advancement and took great risks to achieve these ends. However, others satisfied their expectations simply by having enough autonomy and agency to choose and remain with a partner. Christina van Ambon was one such slavin. When her owners refused to allow her to be with her boyfriend, she disappeared into Batavia's back streets.

Christina had fallen in love with a native burgher, a goldsmith named Samuel Fredrik Brandt. According to the slavin, she began a relationship with Samuel in 1775, and it progressed to the point where they decided to approach her mistress, Sara, about an arrangement that would allow them to be together. Sara and her then-husband, Abraham Walburg, had purchased Christina at an estate sale in 1767 for 100 rijksdaalders, and Christina made it known to Sara that "there was someone who would give 250 rijksdaalders" for her if she were for sale.[29] Sara promised to speak to her husband about it, but Abraham was reluctant to sell Christina and wanted to meet the prospective buyer. Brandt stopped by, and the meeting went at least well enough for Sara to hire Brandt's services as a goldsmith. He repaired two of Sara's silver dog collars, a gold flower hairpin, a pair of "dangling" diamond earrings, and buttons for a *kebaya* (in Malay, a traditional women's blouse), in addition to some rings and a worn-out set of gold buttons belonging to another of Sara's slaves, Malati. The other transaction, however, proved more difficult to negotiate. Seeing their reluctance to sell Christina, Samuel offered to "rent" Christina for five rijksdaalders a month, promising to teach her how to embroider and how to make bridal veils. Despite Brandt's proposals, said Christina, Sara "did not want to listen."[30]

One late morning not long thereafter, Christina went out to a warong and never came back. Brandt was the immediate suspect in the disappearance. The day Christina went missing, Sara sent one of her slaves to Brandt's house, five times, asking after her slavin. After dark Brandt pretended to help look for her but eventually slipped away from the search party. Christina showed up that night at Brandt's brother's house, and a few days later Christina and Samuel moved in together to a small rented hut on the Rua Novo (Portuguese for "New Street"). Meanwhile, Sara's slaves had tracked them to their hut, and sensing the heat the couple moved again, this time to a house adjacent to Brandt's brother's house. By removing back wall panels and sealing his door, Brandt was able to connect the two homes and provide a safe house for him and Christina to live in.[31]

For nineteen months, Christina stayed indoors except for the occasional nighttime trip to the riverbank, her actions more confined in freedom than in slavery. However, her freedom of movement was a sacrifice she was willing to make and was less important than her relationship and future with Brandt. The couple had an impressive run and managed to elude authorities far longer than most runaways did, but even the anonymity of Batavia could not hide Christina forever. Neighbors began to notice something strange about the connected houses. One mentioned "there was a rumor circulating that Brandt had taken a girl from Juff [Dutch for "Miss"], the widow Walburg, and he almost always kept the house locked and went out via his brother's house."[32] Three days before Christmas 1776, acting on a tip from an exceptionally curious neighbor, Sara's nephew, several of her slaves, and two of the bailiff's police raided the safe house.[33] Dulla van Bugis, one of Sara's "boys" or slaves, recalled Christina running between the houses and Brandt's sister-in-law warning him in Portuguese, "Brother, get out of here quick, sissy has been caught."[34]

Under interrogation (possibly torture with a cat-o'-nine-tails), Brandt devised a story about how Christina had appeared at his door just minutes before authorities broke it down, asking him to take her home.[35] When Brandt asked her why she had been gone so long, Christina allegedly told Brandt that her unnamed brother had seduced her into running away, taken her to the highlands, and sold her to "one of the ubiquitous Javanese from Solo."[36] Unfortunately for Brandt, Christina did not have a brother.[37] The aldermen found it "impossible" that he could not have known her whereabouts. "Under his commanding care," it was noted, "she ate, drank, slept and associated with him daily." Drossart of the Batavian environs, Jan Hendrik Trevijn declared that Brandt "was infected with a fetid soul" but "was not content with having debauched his neighbor's lowly slavin with his foul lustings." Beyond that, Brandt had also encouraged her on to "further evil by relinquishing herself from her master's service in an unlawful and derisive manner."[38] By first offering to buy Christina van Ambon outright, then to rent her to Samuel Fredrik Brandt, the couple had exhausted the legal channels for obtaining her freedom. When Christina's master and mistress refused to let her and Samuel live as husband and wife, they resorted to unlawful avenues for social advancement.[39]

Poedak

In court custody at the city surgeon's and bearing a seven-month-old baby in her arms, the slavin Poedak van Buton sat down and related the story of her years on the run as a fugitive, of the man she fell in love with, and of the "child they brought into the world."[40] About two years prior, in 1785, Poedak was a slavin of the native captain Abdul Wahap Soernang when she "became close friends" with a man named Saual. Saual was then stationed as a soldier at the Utrecht Gate, guarding the west entrance to Batavia's city walls; like most rank-and-file soldiers, he was an Asian male. Soon thereafter, Saual gave up soldiering and made his living cutting rice. Poedak and Saual's friendship grew until "after a time," as Poedak described in her statement, they had "intimate relations" and "one night at 3 AM" he "persuaded" Poedak to leave her master and run away with him.[41]

Soldiers were some of the worst paid employees of the Dutch in Asia, and it is unlikely that the poor but passionate soldier-slavin couple fled with much in savings. Unlike many of the other couples, Poedak and Saual conspired only to steal Poedak from her master; the rest of Captain Abdul's property went untouched. The pair's relative privation seems all the more likely given Poedak's description of their subsequent lives as constantly on the move to find work and evade capture. A year after their escape, Poedak gave birth to their child, sometime around June 1786 (we are given no clues as to the sex of the baby). While life could not have been easy for the new family, Poedak claimed that they had always found somewhere to stay and "were always provided for." For two years, they moved from place to place with Saual seeking work, harvesting rice. Perhaps Poedak was looking to get in on January's early harvest of dry rice when they moved to Tanjong on 2 January 1787.

Increasingly in the late seventeenth and eighteenth centuries, most of Batavia's life and growth pulsed outside the very walls over which Saual had stood watch. Villages, towns, estates, and plantations radiated inland from the unhealthy inner city forming Batavia's *Ommelanden* (environs). In Batavia's early days, when the VOC's position on Java was so precarious, the Company either took refuge on the sea or hid behind thick castle walls. Batavia itself was wrested in 1619 from the dependency of the nearby pepper emporium to the west, the sultanate of Banten, throwing the Company into an immediate state of war with Banten's Prince Ranamanggula. Conflict ceased temporarily with the 1624 unseating of Ranamanggula and only came to an end when Banten was brought under effectual Dutch suzerainty in the 1680s.[42] Throughout the 1600s, the Company remained ill at ease with the Javanese, choosing for example to bring in servants and slaves from South Asia, especially Bengal, in the first half of the seventeenth century and from sites in the Indonesian archipelago outside of Java thereafter.[43] Three days after the Company declared war on Banten in July 1656, the ruling Council of the Indies issued an edict declaring that "all the Javanese men, women, and children residing in the city must move out of Batavia and henceforth no more Javanese would be allowed in the city of Batavia." By the end of the month, the High Government would allow no more Javanese to enter the city walls, because, as the Council reasoned, "one can't tell the good from the bad Bantammers [residents of Banten]."[44]

From Batavia's eastern approach, Java's expansionist sultan Agung of Mataram laid siege in the decade after its founding, but in 1628–1629 plague halted his advance just outside the city's walls. Agung notwithstanding, Batavia's environs, especially areas further inland, were considered generally healthier and less malarial than Batavia proper. As the eighteenth-century *pax Neerlandica* eliminated threats from rival Javanese states, the city's population began spreading out toward what became the hill station Buitenzorg (Dutch for "Without Cares").[45] By coming to Tanjong, Poedak and Saual were on the cutting edge of the capital city's endless urban sprawl.

As the Batavian environs were "tamed," the Board of Land Trustees (*Collegie van Heemraden*) ceded huge tracts of land to prominent individuals, a practice mirrored again after 1870 when, on a much grander scale, all of Java went up for sale to private and corporate capital interests. When Poedak and Saual arrived there in early 1787, Tanjong belonged to the former Batavian commissioner van Riemsdijk and was managed by a Javanese foreman named Dul Soekoer. According to Poedak, they stayed with Dul while they arranged for a little piece of land in the *kampung* (Malay for "village"), "to be able to put up a hut and build a house there."[46] Saual said he wanted to "fix up an already-standing hut." Perhaps the couple thought they could settle there with their little baby and stop running. If so, they were mistaken. One morning shortly after their arrival in Tanjong, a former foreman named Bapak Saringtang came by and began "carefully examin[ing]" Saual.[47] When the foremen consulted each other, they realized that Saual had been lying, telling one he hailed from Poelo (Pulau?) Gadong and the other that he was from Crawang. The foremen asked Saual why his story varied, and Bapak Saringtang asked Saual to turn over his large, broad curved-blade *gollok* that he wore at his side.[48] Instead of giving up the knife, explains Poedak, Saual fled, leaving the foremen behind. Several minutes later from the rice paddy to which Poedak had retreated, she saw her husband being escorted back to the village by the foremen and posse, his body trussed, and his head bloodied. According to several witnesses (including Saual), in the escape attempt he had tripped and fallen face first on a rock. Villagers later found Poedak in the paddy and, as bystanders did so often in the criminal records, turned her over to the authorities.

Police hauled the entire family—mother, child, and bloodied father—into the Stadhuis (Dutch, for "city hall") and charged Saual with transporting a slavin and Poedak with running away from her master. Unpunished fugitive slaves and slavinnen posed a serious threat to the older domestic forms of urban bondage and to a newly emerging coolie cultivation system; and in both cases the colonial state through its legislative and judicial systems sought to punish and prevent this and other forms of human capital flight. Therefore, the civil code was decidedly weighted against kidnapper and runaway, but a loophole outlining the nuances in human trafficking was just large enough to allow Saual to slip through the hangman's noose.

Statutes passed by the Hooge Overigheid Deezer Landen (Supreme Government of These Lands, another appellation for the Council of the Indies at Batavia) in 1688 and 1710 set down and further clarified the position that kidnapping was a crime punishable by death, "unless the abducted or trafficked persons are slaves."[49] Kidnapping free persons was a capital offense, but in the case of illegal slave-trafficking, the punishment was left to the discretion of the judges who would weigh the attending circumstances, as to whether they were attenuating or aggravating. Trafficking in persons was a crime against human beings, but trafficking in slaves was a property crime, and the punishments varied accordingly. Saual was sentenced to a "severe flogging" with the cat-o'-nine-tails, a branding, and twenty-five years of hard labor.

Poedak and her child spent the next four and a half months in jail, where they would have witnessed numerous criminal sentences being carried out. Their sunken cell in the back basement of the Stadhuis presented them with a ground-level view of the execution square. On 19 May 1787, the *scherprechter* (Dutch for "executioner") brought Poedak behind the Stadhuis and gave her a "severe rope-lashing" in full view of the spectators.[50] Her punishment, though less physically severe than Saual's, was assigned a higher pedagogic purpose and was intended to be as instructive to her peers as it was to her. According to the aldermen, Poedak "deserve[d] a severe correction so that by her example others may be frightened away from leaving their masters and she will also weigh the consequences of running away again." The court further sentenced Poedak to serve her master for a year in chains and to pay all court costs.[51] Like many slavinnen, Poedak did not cite physical abuse or the institution of slavery itself as the reason for running away. She had simply fallen in love and wanted to start a family. Confined by Batavian property laws and denied what was for her a reasonable expectation, Poedak had decided to take her chances on the run.

Sitie

One of the richest and most detailed cases in the records of the Batavian Court of Aldermen is the 1792 runaway, fraud, and seduction trial of the slavin Sitie van Makasar and the medicine man Kyai Dukun, alias Sitjoe de Wangsa. Serving as the slavin of a Moor, Sheik Nannekoe, Sitie allegedly worked her way into her master's good graces, posed as his concubine, and embezzled a small fortune on his credit line while hoping to set aside a nest egg for her future freedom.[52] Along the way, she claimed, she fell under the spell of a *dukun*, blaming his black magic as the source of her deception. For the prosecution, the case involved tracing the intricate financial web of pawn and credit, "fraud and bamboozling," delving into the "black and dangerous magic" of a "sorcerer," and bringing clarity to the fuzzy relationship between a slavin concubine and an "overly permissive" master.[53]

Sitie van Makasar, as her name implies, was originally from the huge port city on the island of Sulawesi. As the Company's factories and fortifications in Indonesia became less tenuous, Indonesian instead of Indian slaves became more prevalent and Makassar-based slavers combed the eastern archipelago for human chattel to sell at the Batavian slave auctions. Sitie likely met this fate. From her marathon twenty-five-hundred-word interrogation, we learn that Sitie had been with her master, the sheik, for two years and through "good behavior" she had "won his trust"—so much so, in fact, that she governed the entire household, including Sitie's fellow slaves, whom her master had charged to obey Sitie and to be "subjected to her." She also wielded power outside the household including buying and selling on the sheik's credit. According to Sitie, Sheik Nannekoe treated her as "a completely free person" and had given her "the necessary clothing and jewelry" to act as such. In fact, the clothing and jewelry, combined with Nannekoe's treatment and Sitie's deportment, were the enabling conditions in the escape drama that later unfolded. If we can believe what is written in her interrogation, Sitie felt "completely assured" of her future free status and never "entertain[ed] the slightest thought of being unfaithful to him or of leaving his house," until a toothache brought her "the misfortune of falling into the hands" of a Javanese healer named Sitjoe de Wangsa and by whom she was "led astray through his wizardry."

The ordeal began in the summer of 1792 (probably late July), when Sitie sought the services of Sitjoe de Wangsa in hopes of finding a cure for her sore mouth.[54] "On the street," according to court records, people referred to Sitjoe as Kyai Dukun, and witnesses did refer to him by his title rather than his given name. *Kyai* is the Javanese title for a traditional scholar of Islam, but it also has pre-Islamic origins in faith healing, soothsaying, and martial arts.[55] *Dukun* is a Malay term for a medicine man, shaman, or someone who is otherwise a "custodian of specialized esoteric knowledge."[56] Sitjoe seems to have earned his doubly efficacious title of Kyai Dukun; Sitie went looking for him based on word of mouth that he was a "very skillful" healer.[57]

Unable to locate him after a morning spent searching in the Pancoodjang region around Batavia, Sitie was returning home and had stopped off at a warong to buy betel from a woman named Ma Alie, who related to her that a Kyai Dukun had just stopped by her warong. Sitie approached him, and the dukun offered to buy her a cup of coffee at Ma Alie's food stall. Kyai Dukun told Sitie that he had medicine for her mouth, and she accepted his invitation to visit his home in Pisang Batu. The place does sound enchanting. Sitie describes it as replete with "sweet apples and odorous peanuts and many more things." The two were received there by Kyai Dukun's wife, a "very old woman" named Ranati. Despite being treated "very friendly by this couple," when evening fell Sitie wanted to return home. She was probably acutely aware of sections 21 and 22 of the slave statutes, drubbed into the crowd at the public slave castigations: those transporting, hiding, and keeping slaves for up to two meals will be fined, thereafter it is considered kidnapping, with the slaves often judged as co-conspirators.[58]

Kyai Dukun and Ranati must also have known the risks involved in keeping another's slave. They would later argue, as did others, that they had no idea this woman who dressed and acted like a free person was in fact a slavin. However, according to Sitie, Kyai Dukun and Ranati focused on her slave status, becoming more insistent that she spend the night, and began filling her head with ideas and designs against her master. Ranati and the dukun varied their approach. First they targeted Sheik Nannekoe's "Moorness," telling Sitie that she "would be safe with them and that it was better to live with them than with a Moor who as a rule were a bad people and were like unto snakes and upon whom people could not trust." They continued their assault, this time with the level-headed argument about the transitory nature of foreign traders, explaining that Sheik Nannekoe would soon be returning to his homeland, and Sitie would then be sold, so she should "take care of herself now and ideally get a hold of sufficient of her master's money to build a house and many other enticing reasons." Whether it was the dukun's magic or his logic, he convinced Sitie to stay the night. There would be no turning back.

Her toothache was still raging, so Kyai Dukun smeared some medicine on Sitie's head and gave her two documents to wear on her stomach. According to Sitie, Kyai Dukun told her that if she wore the enchanted letters, her master would feel compassion toward her and would be unable to condemn her conduct and behavior. Sitie reported that after this procedure she "felt not the least regard for her master but, in contrast, repeatedly experienced a never before felt urge to be where the dukun was." Sitie not only spent the night, she spent eight nights there before returning to her legal master Sheik Nannekoe, though in spirit Sitie was serving a new master with powerful magic. Sheik Nannekoe issued no fugitive slave warrant while she was away and accepted her into the household when she came back on her own. This is not surprising, since his testimony suggests that while he may have purchased her as a slavin, at the time of her flight Sheik Nannekoe viewed Sitie as "now his concubine" whom he "held in very high trust."[59] He had come to see her not as his chattel, but while her situation with Sheik Nannekoe, even after her first absence, was "good," she was "unable to stand staying there." Sitie said she felt mysteriously "pressed" and "could find no rest" until she was reunited with the dukun and shortly after her return she ran away a second time to be with him.

With the next runaway episode, the dukun had increased his hold, and Sitie's absence increased from eight nights to thirty. In this world where class and identity were flexible (despite statutory wishes) and could change with one's wardrobe, it was not difficult for Sitie to appear as anything she wanted, though the law made it more difficult to change that appearance into juridical reality. One afternoon, Sitie left Nannekoe for the second time and went to the house of an unnamed woman but found no one home. Sitie had arrived in style in a covered perahu and a neighbor woman named Ma Aijo took Sitie in.[60] She stayed the night at Ma Aijo's before proceeding on to the dukun's. Several days later Sitie returned to Ma Aijo's with rice, fish, and betel thanking her for her hospitality. Ma Aijo hosted her for a little over a week, loaning Sitie two sarongs. Finally, Sheik Nannekoe learned of her whereabouts and sent "a trusted Moor," Abdul Rachman, and a Makassarese boy in a wagon to pick her up. In her statement, Ma Aijo, like most of the other witnesses was oblivious to Sitie's legal status as a slavin, having "no idea" said Ma Aijo, "that Sitie was doing this without her master's permission, with whom Sitie lived as a concubine [*goendik*; in Malay, *gundik*, synonym for concubine]." As further proof of Ma Aijo's unawareness, when Sitie left in Nannekoe's wagon, Ma loaned her three more sarongs telling Sitie that she could hold onto them until she returned. A third escape came shortly thereafter with Sitie returning on her own after four days. On her fourth attempt, the law stepped in, and there would be no more running away.

The next few months were tempestuous for Sitie. By her version of events, she was torn between her masters, running away four times, each time blaming the irresistible urge to be at Kyai Dukun's where she was ordered to steal, propositioned to marry, and encouraged to murder. According to Sitie, Kyai Dukun would make frequent trips into the city to spy on Sheik Nannekoe, waiting until he was away. Then Kyai Dukun would bring Sitie word, telling her to go home and gather up whatever valuables she could lay her hands on so that he could be "in a position to build or buy a house" for her. Ranati is said also to have told Sitie that "her husband should marry such a woman" as Sitie, because Ranati, citing her own age, "was an old person and would want her husband to have no one more than Sitie."[61] Although she felt a mysterious attraction to the medicine man, Sitie said she was never tempted to marry Kyai Dukun. Stated in retrospect and transcribed in the third person, Sitie questioned herself: "Why couldn't she leave the dukun if she saw in him a man for whom she could foster no love," when there were so many things "more worth her love?" She continued to wonder, "Why then, did she not treat [his advances] with disdain when he once violently tried to kiss her?"

Sitie said that ever since the dukun had cast his spell over her, "from that time forward [she] felt not the least regard" for Sheik Nannekoe. This is questionable, however. For example, Kyai Dukun tried to persuade her to take Nannekoe's things. We will later delve into Sitie's financial misconduct, but when she fleeced her own home at Kyai Dukun's bidding, she never took Sheik Nannekoe's belongings, only her own clothing and jewelry. Kyai Dukun also suggested that through murder, Sitie could be free of her master and could live with the dukun alone, but Sitie rejected "with revulsion" the dukun's proposition that she "help her master over the edge." It is impossible to calculate the point at which Sitie's agency ended and the dukun's control began. But he tipped that balance in his favor by appealing to two slave aspirations manifest again and again in the testimonies given by runaways: stable, long-term love and the nest egg to support it. We have already seen how Sitie spurned Kyai Dukun's advances (although she was still brought to tears by her "longing and emotion" for him), but she moved aggressively to make that second dream a reality.

With considerable style and skill, Sitie lit up Batavia's bazaars, pawn-shops, and boutiques with Sheik Nannekoe's formidable credit line. Three things made this possible: Nannekoe's influence, Sitie's connection to it and amplification of it, and the prevalence of women in the marketplace. Nannekoe was a respected merchant about town, and his public treatment of Sitie as a free person or at the very least as his concubine afforded her the requisite credibility to be able to pull off her spending spree. Nyai Janna, a "free Malay" and an illiterate Muslim businesswoman, described a visit the couple had made to her house seventeen months prior.[62] Janna described Sitie as "dressed in the attire and the sophistication of a free woman," and Janna became acquainted with Sitie as the concubine, not the slavin, of the "Moor Nannekoe." So, three months later when Sitie came, "wearing and acting" the same (that is, free and rich) in addition to being attended by two slavinnen in a retinue, Nyai Janna accepted, without contest, that the "concubine" was fully authorized to traffic in Nannekoe's name.

The sheik had unwittingly played an important part in the con by being seen with and by treating Sitie as his equal. It was, however, her attention to detail and dramatic flair that enabled her to operate under the radar by making such an obvious spectacle of herself. The idea of the accompanying entourage was a brilliant gesture on Sitie's part and would have rendered her immediately recognizable as a woman of unquestioned consequence.[63] Sitie did not deny the allegation of a slavin retinue. When questioned, she said that she often took the slave girls with her for the day to "show them off" when she went somewhere "acting like a woman of privilege."[64] After Sitie's grand entrance with her entourage of slavinnen , she asked Janna if she could rent a gold medallion, eighteen gold buttons, and a black kabaya. Janna was in the business of helping Batavia's social climbers afford their adornments by renting them out to others when not in use. Sitie said she needed the things to attend a wedding in style, and Nyai Janna rented them to her for three rijksdaalders. In terms of rijksdaalders, the transaction with Nyai Janna was one of the least expensive of Sitie's many excursions with Nannekoe's credit, but it would prove one of the most costly for Sitie.

Sitie's finery and entourage were a necessary part of her cover and helped her, on another occasion, to leverage wealth, credit, and prestige. On 5 October 1792, a Moor named Pier Mochaman testified that, several months prior, Sitie had visited his home shop, offering to sell three slave girls to him. The asking price, according to Pier, was too high, and "thus nothing came of that transaction." How meteoric must have been Sitie's rise to power if she could be bold enough to sell fellow slavinnen without their objection? Can we even call her a slavin when everyone inside and outside her household treated her as something more than that? The law, however, had a different perspective. It is precisely this disjuncture between the statutory definition and the social reality (and, of course, her buying spree) that landed Sitie in so much trouble.

Although her bid to sell the slave girls to Mochaman was unsuccessful, it put her on the merchant's radar as a person of means who drove a hard bargain. When Sitie returned three days later with "her" three slavinnen to purchase two sets of gold buttons for thirty rijksdaalders, Mochaman assumed that her standing was legitimate. Her attempted sale of the slavinnen may have been an elaborate ruse, orchestrated to ingratiate herself with Mochaman while holding onto the slavinnen who were a necessary part of the fraud. Mochaman's trust was not won easily, however. He asked her to pay for the gold buttons on the spot. Sitie asked him to extend her credit, informing him that she lived with a Moor in his house on the Pajagalan. Mochaman agreed, but as further insurance he sent one of his own slaves to follow her home to see if the story checked out. It did.

Winning Mochaman's hard-earned trust paid additional dividends. Based on his word, a neighboring merchant also allowed Sitie to take home valuable luxury items on favorable terms. In court, the neighbor, a Moor named Mochamat Tsikini, testified that sometime around June 1792 "a certain finely-dressed native woman followed by three slave girls" came to his house asking what he had for sale. Tsikini laid out a few things for her. Sitie chose a Bengalese chintz, a long *kust* (Dutch for "coast") garment, and two batik handkerchiefs. The total came to twelve and a quarter rijksdaalders. Sitie paid one rijksdaalder and six stivers and took the rest on Nannekoe's account, agreeing to return with cash. In his statement Mochamat Tsikini said that he trusted her, because Pier Mochaman knew where she lived and had sold her things on credit. True to her word, in part, Sitie did return the next day, Tsikini reported—not with cash to settle her debts but with a shopping list to incur more. Tsikini obliged, and Sitie bought a textile with supplementary gold weft (*songket*) for twenty rijksdaalders and a handkerchief for nine and three-quarters rijksdaalders, bringing her grand total with Tsikini to forty rijksdaalders and forty-two stivers.

Following Sitie's trail through the market and bazaars of Batavia demonstrates the richness and diversity of its many mixed ethnic communities. Seeking out her own roots, Sitie used Nannekoe's credit line to purchase twenty-four Makassarese sarongs from a Makassarese merchant for sixty-six rijksdaalders. Her origins probably gave her specialized knowledge from which to judge the textiles of her homeland. Sitie later sold several of these back to the aforementioned Moor, Mochamat Tsikini. Sitie also turned a handsome profit trading through Batavia's ubiquitous Chinese pawnshops. One peranakan Chinese merchant, Bapak Salee, described how a "certain well dressed and reputable/estimable female" (the clerk, Johanes Lohr, added "or so she appeared to him") came to his store to pawn a silver betel container and later two textiles, one bearing the familiar gold weft. Bapak Salee gave her fifty rijksdaalders and warned her that the goods might move quickly, as he would be handing them over to another pawnbroker who was anxious to return to China. Salee knew neither that he was buying stolen merchandise nor that Sitie did not intend to get them out of hock.

From another Chinese broker, we also learn that Sitie occasionally used an alias, but she always added the name she used with the title *Nyai*. Oeij Loanko, who moonlighted as a scribe, told the aldermen about a "very well-dressed woman," whom on sight he took for a free person, who brought gold-woven textiles (*songket*) and pawned them under the name Nyai Daliema for seven rijksdaalders.[65] Another "scribe," Na Kienseeng, related a similar scenario when "a certain eminently attired female, calling herself 'Nyai Sitie'" came into the pawnshop run by Na Kienseeng (a Chinese man named Lie Tsjongko was the shop owner) and pawned two unsewn sarongs for three and a half rijksdaalders, four days later pawning two more for three rijksdaalders.

Established shops and merchants were not the only place to do business in Batavia. Then, as now, a labyrinthine network of market stalls and private homes and individuals formed an important part of its commercial landscape. Nyai Janna was one such example of an individual meeting a consumer need that fell just between the cracks of the business establishment. In Janna's case, it was creating a way for individuals to make money off their property while not risking their ownership of it, a safer and less permanent alternative than selling or pawning. Slaves, even those recognized as such by both the law and the community, were also a vibrant part of this commercial tapestry.

A slavin named Jamia testified about her business dealings with "Nyai Sitie." Her statement was an example of the slow early-late modern transition of Southeast Asia's underclass from upwardly mobile slaves and bondservants to permanent coolies. It is important to note that those nineteenth-century preoccupations with the abolition of slavery, especially in the colonies, were not ultimately pinned on moral or ethical foundations, despite the moral and ethical arguments marshaled in abolition's behalf. Slaves and their care and upkeep were expensive, much more so than a "self-sustaining" population of coolie laborers. Furthermore, the close, often domestic or even familial connections between slaves and their masters and mistresses were no longer in keeping with the impersonal, purely economic nature of colonial corvee, plantation, and coolie wage slavery. In this important transition between the patron-client relationship of the old and the industrial relationship of the new era, we find underclass slaves straddling that line: forming a part of an extended household but also expected to bring home what was known as "coolie money" by working on the outside. Jamia, a slavin of the former captain of the Chinese in Batavia, describes how every month she was to earn four rupees coolie money. Unlike many of her eighteenth-century peers and nearly all of her nineteenth-century peers, the enterprising slavin was able to find coolie money without resorting to arduous plantation labor. Jamia obtained permission from her master and became a low-level pawnbroker. Through Jamia, Sitie pawned several items, including one sewn and one unsewn sarong, which (not surprisingly) Sitie did not claim and Jamia went on to sell.

With her buying and selling spree in high gear and creditors calling on Sheik Nannekoe to settle his own debts, Sitie was now permanently on the run from her master. She would soon have to account for her deeds. Like so many of the civil and criminal disputes in Batavia, a combination of the municipal government and citizen vigilantes carried out the investigation, the arrest, and occasionally the interrogation. Two weeks after her last visit to Nyai Janna, Sitie returned to the businesswoman, sans jewelry, and asked for another week's extension, which Janna granted. Not surprisingly, Janna was livid when she found that Sitie had since gone away without leave and she realized that she had "no real recourse while Sitie was missing." Since then, Nyai Janna was on the lookout for Sitie and fatefully bumped into her on the street one day. She detained Sitie and demanded that they go see Steven Poelman, chief prosecutor of the Batavian environs.[66]

On 1 October 1792, Poelman filed a criminal brief before the president of the Court of Aldermen, Johannes Siberg, bringing formal charges against Sitie and Kyai Dukun.[67] Listing her by her full legal name and title, the brief charged "the slavin Sitie van Makasar belonging to the Moor Sheik Nannekoe" with endangering Nannekoe's property (including Sitie herself) and with "other crimes."[68] Although Sitie had accumulated a sizeable nest egg, she had squandered much of it. According to Sitie, much of what she collected went to Kyai Dukun.[69] Nyai Janna's allegations would have been enough to have those charges filed against Sitie, but the addition to the brief of Sitjoe de Wangsa, alias Kyai Dukun, meant that there must have been an undocumented interrogation of Sitie between her arrest and the October 1 arraignment. Days later, on October 5, we find the record of Sitie's formal examination, undoubtedly a long day, as all involved with the trial, which included no fewer than thirteen defendants and witnesses, were brought into court to testify and potentially face off against each other on any discrepancies in their statements. In addition to the lengthy interrogation report, Sitie was made to confront Nyai Janna, Ma Aaijo, Mochaman Tsikini, Bapak Salee, Oeij Loanko, Na Kienseeng, and Jamia in turn.

The dukun pleaded innocent of wrongdoing and ignorant of Sitie's slave status, and his eighty-year-old wife, Ranati, did likewise.[70] He claimed that he made a simple living by dealing in medicine or as a practicing physician. When asked to identify Sitie, Kyai Dukun claimed only to know her because he met her once by the Jassenbrug by Ma Alie's house. According to Kyai Dukun, he never knew that she was a slavin. Sitie claimed simply to have had a fever and needed medicine, so she accompanied him to his house and stayed two days with a short visit later.[71]

Sitie was alone in characterizing Kyai Dukun as malefactor, but the picture she painted of witchcraft and manipulation of women was bleak enough to cast a shadow of suspicion over him. "During the time they lived together, she noticed how much power this dukun had over others and by conducting his magic arts and means of sorcery various women or *nyonyas* came to him to partake of his good advice and support so that the women folk were chained to him and with no effort he could entice [them] to do his bidding." When "company of this sort" would arrive, Kyai Dukun would send Sitie upstairs, so she "never had the opportunity to spy upon the reasons and results of their visits whether they occupied themselves with games or came for medicine and were very familiar." Kyai Dukun, said Sitie, was well-known as a "person who could perform sorcery" and who "knew how to bring the strangest affairs in order." Even though her imprisonment and interrogation had afforded Sitie distance from and critical perspective on Kyai Dukun, his power over her remained visible even from her jail cell, where she said that the dukun helped her a lot with her dreams and her sadness, and that she "still felt this longing and emotion for him and even now in prison cannot think about him without breaking into tears."[72]

The medicine man said he only loaned her five rijksdaalders, and she pawned several items to him in return. Kyai Dukun denied all wrong-doing, but several pieces of evidence matched Sitie's story and tied him to the crime. Two weeks after Kyai Dukun's interrogation, when as was customary he was read back his earlier statement and asked to attest to its truthfulness, new facts were presented to him, and he had to account for them. The most damning revelation was a pair of gold buttons found in the jail's garbage pile that bore a striking resemblance to some of the missing buttons in question. When pressed, the dukun said that he had been wearing those buttons on his shirt when he arrived in jail but had subsequently misplaced them. Sitie had testified that the Kyai Dukun had smeared some medicine on her head and gave her two charmed letters that would make Nannekoe sympathetic and accepting. Later, when the medicine man landed in jail and was searched by the guards, the officers reported finding a tightly folded "Malay document" bound to his body. Although the court tacitly acknowledged his supernatural powers, the magic charm did not elicit the desired sympathy and acceptance from his jailers.[73] The aldermen convicted Sitjoe de Wangsa, alias Kyai Dukun, of seducing Sitie into running away and sentenced him to pay court costs, to "toil on the public works" for fifteen years, and thereafter to be banished from Batavia.

In its final ruling the court was particularly concerned with Sitie's path from slavin to free-spending nyai. Sheik Nannekoe had made good most of the financial losses, and so this case, according to drossart Poelman, was less a cautionary tale of fraud than of slave impudence.[74] "Under the guise of a free person," said Poelman, Sitie "played her various roles at the expense of her master's bankroll" but was able to do so only because she had been given "sufficient opportunity" to significantly expand the power Nannekoe had given her.[75]

Sitie's story is an example of the clash of one notion of status and mobility with a legal system that had been set up to keep people in their place. Following the fluid Southeast Asian model, we see a slavin working her way up within her master's household, being given command over Nannekoe's many slaves and retainers, and eventually becoming the sheik's trusted partner, lover, and equal. But according to Roman Dutch law and the jurists and aldermen assigned to her case, under the law Sitie was just a slavin, and her meteoric rise to the top of the household had not changed this essential fact. For her crimes the aldermen ordered Sitie to be bound to a pole, beaten severely with rods on the bare back, confined to chains, sent to toil on the public works for fifteen years, and thereafter to be banned, in addition to paying court costs.

Poelman assigned part of the blame to Nannekoe. In the eyes of the court, her master had "grant[ed] her too much authority," and his failure to treat her as a slavin "was essentially behind the misdeed . . . put[ting] her in a certain mindset so that she was able to conduct herself as a free person . . . and as a free person [she] stepped outside the boundaries of sincerity and good faith and through cunning and deceitful ways bilked others of their property."[76] Why would the aldermen find this "certain mindset" problematic? We should not assume that the aldermen were opposed to social climbing in principle—first, because the aldermen themselves had scrambled up to their station by outliving and outplaying other claimants, and second, because abstract moral principles were rarely a deciding factor in the colonies. For the municipal authorities, it was not so much that they possessed a clear, civilizing mission statement or that they lay awake nights brooding over the morals and mores of their constituency. On the contrary, it was often the VOC's blatant amorality that made it so successful. Instead, what probably bothered civil authorities was that Sitie and Sheik Nannekoe's behavior threatened one of the basic assumptions of the international merchant community in Batavia: that local laws would ensure their property could not arbitrarily run away.

Esperanca

Esperanca van Bugis was a slavin of the notary Karel Kuvel and his wife. Drawing on an underclass network of friends and lovers, Esperanca and a fellow slavin, Isabelle van Timor, attempted a hastily planned and executed escape from their Dutch master and mistress that landed them before the Schepenbank. Esperanca was many things to many people, wife, concubine, slavin, defendant, and her story helps explain the conflict between the situational nature of class, status, and identity on the streets of Batavia and the unbending rule of law in its courtrooms. The tension this conflict produced drove many slavinnen to run the legal gauntlet on their flight from their legal masters.

A major point of divergence between Southeast Asian commercial centers and their competing European commercial enterprises was the absence, in Southeast Asia, of clear safeguards for private property.[77] Those safeguards found, for example, in Dutch-controlled enclaves were an important part of the enclaves' economic success, but that success (and the law code it required) had different social consequences. Its maintenance required an exacting juridical architecture that narrowly categorized individuals as either free or slave. Merchants, especially international sojourners, needed the security and assurance that their property, human and otherwise, was guaranteed until their departure, and that their slaves could not simply walk away when they had fulfilled some vague sense of debt obligation. The constrictions that the statutory code placed on traditional social fluidity closed off other avenues for movement and flux within the urban setting. Painted as slavinnen in perpetuity (and, legally speaking, into such a tight corner), many women chose to take their chances as fugitives in the hopes of upward advancement.

Like Sitie van Makasar, Esperanca van Bugis was also from the island of Sulawesi. In the previous century, Sitie and Esperanca's ancestors had squared off against each other in an important series of wars, whose resolution spelled the end of the last serious contest to Dutch authority in the archipelago. Since the fall of Melaka to the Portuguese in 1511, Makassar had become an increasingly important hub in the international spice trade and long-distance bulk trade. Larger than Amsterdam and filled with international trading vessels, Makassar posed a real threat to Dutch monopolistic designs in the region. In 1666 the VOC allied with the nearby rival seafaring kingdom of the Bugis, and Makassar finally fell in 1669. This accelerated a diaspora of Bugis from Wajo who had sided with Makassar and increased instability and slave raiding in eastern Indonesia, the likely origin of Sitie and Esperanca's condition as slavinnen from the island of Sulawesi.

From the written record, it is difficult to know exactly who Esperanca was. She had been bought and sold on the slave market several times and was unhappy in her current state. One day after her Dutch master Karel Kuvel castigated her, Esperanca became desperate enough to do something about it. Kuvel lived in Batavia's kampung Gatiep, and two Javanese stablemen, Panjang and Serijam, looked after his horses. It was there where Panjang said he "came to know" Esperanca and "lived in concubinage" with her.[78] Panjang said that, after her run-in with Kuvel, Esperanca had asked him to take her away. He admitted that he wanted to bring her to the uplands and make her his wife. His friend Serijam also confirmed that there was an amorous relationship between Esperanca and Panjang but described it in slightly different terms. According to Serijam, even before the escape Panjang spoke of her as his wife. In his confession, Serijam related a critical conversation in which Panjang "said that his wife Esperanca wanted to be taken away." Esperanca's testimony also does not clear up the matter. She refers to Panjang simply as her lover. There was a great deal of slippage in the relationship continuum, and the defendants employed a variety of titles to describe their perception of that affinity. At times she was a slavin, other times a wife, a lover, and sometimes all three. Meanwhile the Court of Aldermen refused to see her as anything but a slavin and never wavered in their insistence on this essential, all-encompassing designation.

As the aldermen describe it in their conclusion, their case was open and shut. Two slavinnen, Esperanca and Isabelle, conspired with two former stablemen to run away from their master, Karel Kuvel. On their way out, the slavinnen stole a chest full of valuables from Kuvel and fled until villagers at the Tanah Abang market outside the city apprehended them. The court also made it clear that the free men would be treated no differently from the slavinnen, "since the first two, although not slaves, were equal participants with the later two, the first shall receive the same harsh punishment as the last."[79]

Other factors, however, show that the case was less than straightforward. In the first place, Batavia was the home to a relatively swift brand of justice, with the Schepenbank usually wrapping up investigation, trial, and sentencing within two months of the arrest. Esperanca and Isabelle were arrested and arraigned on 10 May 1792, but their sentence was not carried out until more than seven months later, in December, a point that a second irregularity may explain. Isabelle was arrested as a co-conspirator, but her "stubborn denial of being an accessory" to the crime seems to have held up the legal proceedings.[80]

Roman Dutch law required a confession for the death sentence and other heavy punishments, to say nothing of the advantages of prosecuting a case with a confession in hand. Torture was the means of "bringing around" a defendant who was less than forthcoming about his or her guilt. On 7 June 1792, we have a record of a confession from everyone on trial except Isabelle. That same day three aldermen interrogated her, but she continued to deny her involvement in the escape plot, pleading her innocence. Then on 25 November 1792 (not long before sentencing), a death certificate for the Timorese slavin Isabelle was registered. It stated that she had been ill since 26 July and had finally succumbed to illness in late November. When Isabelle did not confess, she was tortured. She did not die the day she was tortured, but weeks after her death the head prosecutor, Steven Poelman, announced that they would be moving ahead with the trial. "Notwithstanding Isabelle's contrary testimony," Poelman stated, "the ruling in this case is to be based on the testimony of the other three." Isabelle would no longer be a hindrance.

In the absence of Isabelle's confession, Esperanca provided most of the story line. According to Esperanca, Panjang and Serijam had proposed helping her escape from an abusive household, but she refused. Her master subsequently moved outside Batavia's city gate, Nieuwpoort, and so the stablemen, who lived at the home of a Chinese female warong keeper, were no longer able to work for Kuvel.[81] Nevertheless, Panjang visited his wife/concubine/lover frequently at her new home and in the streets, talking with her "about innocuous subjects."[82] Then one day Esperanca said she met Panjang at a nearby warong, and he asked if she wanted to run away immediately. She refused, and Panjang allegedly pressured her, saying that Isabelle had already accepted the offer. "Wanting to be with them," Esperanca explained, she also agreed to run away.

The next day when Isabelle returned at three o'clock from her errands at the warong, she purportedly told Esperanca that Panjang was there waiting for them. In a heated exchange, Esperanca said she was not willing to do it, while Isabelle "maintained her resolve," telling Esperanca that she was taking some valuables with her as well. Then their master, the Dutch notary Kuvel, returned home. He demanded a sandwich, "but since they lacked the necessary items to make a sandwich," according to Esperanca, she went upstairs to fetch some money from Kuvel's wife.[83] When she came back down, Isabelle had stolen a small writing chest. She gave it to Esperanca who took the chest out back and set it behind the door. Esperanca was now a part of the crime.

She said she gave two other slaves the money to go buy bread and butter, then she went and waited outside the upstairs window. Isabelle threw down one of their mistress's sarongs wrapped in a boy's scarf with gold pendants. Esperanca grabbed more of her mistress's clothing and a long shirt from a fellow slavin named Minerva and gave everything to Panjang and Serijam who were waiting at the back door. Again according to Esperanca, Isabelle waited behind as Esperanca and the stablemen departed, planning to meet up where Isabelle had stashed more of the mistress's valuables. Apparently, Isabelle had an adopted mother living in Manga Dua where she could keep things. For some reason, instead of meeting Isabelle, the three made their way to the Chinese cemetery where Panjang and Serijam smashed open the chest with hatchets (*gollok*) and took out the money, while Esperanca changed into her mistress's kabaya to be less conspicuous. It did not work, for when they arrived at the market at Tanah Abang, they were immediately questioned and apprehended by the locals and brought to the European mandor (foreman) who ran that sprawling estate of Indies' Council member Willem Vincent Helvetius van Riemsdijk. When he searched Esperanca, the mandor found fifty-five and a half rijksdaalders including twenty-four stivers she was also carrying for Serijam. The foreman accused Esperanca of "impersonating a native" and made her tell him whom she belonged to. The runaway slavin and those traveling with the fugitive all ended up in jail.

Isabelle reunited with Esperanca, Panjang, and Serijam in prison. Her story before she died was that she simply went out looking for Esperanca and came back to Kuvel's at nine o'clock after retrieving a sarong to wash on loan from a warong. The Kuvels claimed it was more like ten o'clock when Isabelle arrived home, appearing "very disconcerted" and bearing a dirty old garment.[84] The notary and his wife said that they had been away from seven to half past nine when they returned to find the chest missing. When questioned by her masters, Isabelle said she had been out looking for Esperanca on the plantation estate of a *predikant* (Dutch for "preacher"), and that the garment she was trying to hide behind her back had been given her by a couple of friends in the Manga Dua. Her version of events might have been more plausible had it not been for a couple who identified Isabelle squatting under a mango tree. Abdul and Slamien testified that, as they were heading down to the river on the night in question, they saw Isabelle and asked her what she was doing. She reportedly replied, "I left my master's house to come here and look for Esperanca." Abdul said he sent her away because of the edict against slaves drifting at night and advised her to "get yourself out of here and back to your master's, so that you don't get picked up."[85]

On 17 December 1792, the aldermen assembled the prisoners, minus Isabelle, and read their sentences to them in Malay. They pleaded for mercy, but Steven Poelman stuck with the conclusion he had just penned. The executioner would carry out the sentences that same day. In a response similar to Sitie's case, the aldermen decried the "enemy within" element of runaway slavinnen and domestic theft. "Crimen furtum domesticum," they wrote, "is a crime of the highest order perpetrated by slaves against the property of their legal master," and they continued with a lengthy discussion about the degree to which domestic theft (by servants or slaves) was worse than normal theft.[86] Sitie and Esperanca had intimate knowledge of and access to the household and not only had stolen their owners' valuables but, by running away, had escaped with a considerable amount of human property. Both cases in close proximity would have been weighing on the minds of the jurists.[87] Panjang and Serijam were flogged in public, branded, put in chains, and sentenced to fifty years of hard labor.

As for Esperanca, the aldermen wrote that they hoped her punishment would be an example to other slaves contemplating such actions and would address the growing problem of lawlessness among the slave class. "Such unfaithfulness," they stated, "occurs so often in slaves that one can expect an exemplary and preemptive punishment as the only means one has of impressing others as much as possible with such a deterrent."[88] Esperanca's story is another example of the unwillingness of the state to see individuals outside their statutory position. Esperanca described herself as a lover, vis-à-vis Panjang, while others described her as a concubine and wife. In reality, her social standing was situational and reassessed on a case-by-case basis, but the international commercial capital was unable to manage these fuzzy and shifting interpretations. What mattered to the aldermen was that she was a slavin.

*I*n his edited volume on slavery in Southeast Asia, Anthony Reid argues that only a strong state in an urban setting could "impose a uniform legal system on [its] inhabitants." Indeed, the early modern period was marked by increasingly absolutist and monopolistic states, able to set in statute an iron vision of the great chain of being and, more important, to police it. In Batavia, where not only a strong state governed but also a cosmopolitan merchant population thrived, authorities opted for significant consolidation of and uniformity in the legal system. The law attempted to remove plasticity from urban social relations and to secure the permanent position of slaves. Instead it increased the friction. Urban slave statutes, according to Reid, "created an abstract status of slave as opposed to free, with a juridically defined position as inferior chattels," a position not seen in the countryside.[89]

Rather than assuming their state-assigned role in society as property, many triangulated their status based on the social cues in their immediate vicinity. For example, Sheik Nannekoe and his household did not treat Sitie according to her legal classification as a slavin, and barring her run-in with the dukun, she would have lived out her life as the functional equivalent of a free person. The state punished her less for being a thief (Nannekoe had repaid her debts) than for being an out-of-control slavin. Sitie's story and others highlight the collision of a fluid form of social hierarchy with Batavia's fixed juridical arrangement. True to their civil law tradition, when the aldermen passed judgment on Sitie they did not base their decision on the immediate reality—that Sitie lived the life of a free person—but referred instead to the code that defined Sitie as a slavin.

Other women faced the opposite problem. Their owners shared the state's vision of them as pure property. The firm classification of slave versus non-slave substituted a rigid dichotomy for what had previously been a rough approximation on a sliding scale of "freedom." Many slavinnen did not share their owners' assumptions, resulting in their running away. Impatient ones, such as Danie and Esperanca, hastily seized dangerous opportunities to advance their static lives. Christina, for example, made lawful attempts to pursue a family relationship and only chose to run when her owners proved inflexible. So, while Batavia offered networks and contacts that enabled these women to escape into a new life, on the other hand it also created the problems from which they were running.

GENDER, ABUSE,

AND THE MODERN WORLD SYSTEM

Female Violence in Eighteenth-century Jakarta

The demographic constraints and financial priorities of the Dutch East India Company that brought some Asian women into its "family" also brought the rest of the Asian women in the colonies under its legal authority. The following cases focus on women who abused their inferiors. Either the violence they meted out or the responses it invoked landed them in court, along with a host of witnesses and co-defendants, to tell their stories. These stories demonstrate an important tension within colonial society and highlight a critical moment in the modern world economic system. The shift from the spice economy to the plantation economy tore away the "sentimental veil" from the familial relationships between slave and master, slavin and mistress, and "reduced the family relation into a mere money relation."[1] Slaves and slavinnen who had once been incorporated into the lower rungs of the family ladder were kept at bay. Masters and mistresses no longer felt vertically bonded with their subjects in terms of reciprocal relationships of dependency. Instead, their interests in their underlings had come to rest in notions more connected to chattel ownership, and their behavior followed suit.

The occasional woman from the Asian underclass resorted to excessive violence when dealing with the men and women who were her social inferiors and ended up telling her story to the Court of Aldermen. The following cases of female violence share important traits, clues about the construction of female violence in Batavia. First, regardless of their own status, the women usually abused their social underlings. Second, this almost always happened against someone who performed his or her compensatory labor outside the household: a coolie slave or slavin. Third, if their abuse was "continual" and extreme, as opposed to occasional and fair (if unpleasant), slaves and slavinnen could be pushed over the brink. Fourth, when the victims could no longer bear the abuse, there initiated a gendered response from the men and women, who fought back in very different ways. By comparing six cases similar to Tjindra's (the very first case presented in this study), not only are we given a glimpse of the early plantation economy, we also gain insight into the nature of female violence in a slave society and the construction of gender and mistress-slavin relationships in an early colonial context. More broadly, we are allowed an intimate look at what life was like for underclass women in an early Southeast Asian urban setting, specifically the poor women, slavinnen and concubines, in Indonesia.

CASES OF FEMALE VIOLENCE

Oetan and Tjindra

This book began with a fragment from the tale of misery involving the slavin Tjindra van Bali, who, when near death, recounted a gruesome tale of abuse meted out by her mistress, the Chinese mestiza Oetan. In a normal criminal proceeding, Tjindra would have delivered a formal deposition as soon as possible after the incident. As an indication of the severity of the beating, Tjindra was not well enough to testify for a full week. When she did, she told a sad story of her life as a coolie slavin.[2] She was the slavin of a Malay named Machmat, and every day her master's wife, Oetan, ordered her out of the house to go find work as a coolie, forcing her to earn a daily wage.[3] When she returned empty-handed having been unable to find work, Oetan would beat her with a rattan cane. Unfortunately, according to Tjindra, even when she found work Oetan would still beat her "black and blue, cruelly and severely . . . with rattan or with anything she could get her hands on."[4] Finally when she could take it no longer, Tjindra ran away from her master's house and was quickly picked up by the authorities as a fugitive.

Nearly a month went by before Tjindra's mistress, Oetan, was brought in for questioning. The indictment stated that "the defendant did not punish the aforementioned Tjindra van Bali pursuant to the powers accorded a master or mistress under the law."[5] The late eighteenth-century state was taking an increasing interest in protecting the valuable property that was coolie labor. When pressed under interrogation, Oetan remembered things differently than Tjindra did. One striking difference in their accounts was the ethnicity of Oetan's husband, Tjindra's master. According to Oetan, her husband was a Balinese named Amat.[6] Tjindra was herself Balinese, and twice, to the surgeon and to the court clerks, she refers to Oetan's husband as "a Malay named Mochamat [Machmat]."[7] Whatever his ethnicity, Amat had purchased Tjindra as a gift to honor Oetan at their wedding. A source of honor, Tjindra was also meant to be a source of independent revenue for Oetan. The enterprising mistress could send her slavin out to find work, and despite the fact that Tjindra "was constantly coming home with one day five and the next day four stivers," Oetan "managed to remain calm," she says of herself.[8]

On good days, reported the mistress, Tjindra would come home with a pittance. Oetan remembers Tjindra constantly staying out late when she would send her to the market stalls or on errands. The breaking point finally came when Tjindra came home one day "a filthy mess" (probably from working all day as a coolie slavin), and Oetan admitted using a rattan to hit her, ordering the slavin to go clean off. Tjindra was gone too long bathing, and this made Oetan so furious that she hit her again "a time or two" with the rattan. Then the unthinkable happened for Oetan. Tjindra stood up to her, verbally "brutalizing" Oetan, who then turned up the abuse. She admitted that she took off her slipper and "gave the girl a few smacks on the cheek," but she specifically denied hitting her with firewood or other things. That night Tjindra chose the way out most commonly followed by slavinnen who could stand no more—she ran away.

Thanks to an interesting convention of Roman Dutch law, we are provided with more strange revelations about the abuses suffered by Tjindra. People with conflicting testimonies were often brought face-to-face to confront the differences in their stories. So, on 26 May 1775, four days after Oetan's interrogation and a month after Tjindra's last beating, the two squared off at the courthouse in Batavia.[9] Tjindra showed Oetan her torn left ear. Oetan denied doing it, saying that Tjindra's ear "had long been like that." Then, in one of most bizarre episodes of female violence, Tjindra displayed her ghastly eyelid, accusing Oetan of yanking out a group of her eyelashes. Oetan's reply? She had pulled on them simply to wake Tjindra up because she was in such a deep sleep. This remark may have cost Oetan a slavin. In the sentence convicting her of mistreating Tjindra, lead prosecutor Jan Hendrik Poock was particularly shocked by this act of violence, which clearly crossed the line, even for a mistress, between discipline and torture.[10]

The court declared Oetan guilty. How would they punish her without upsetting the social order of things? Oetan was, after all, a mistress and Tjindra a slavin. Had the roles been reversed and the slavin tortured the mistress (though those roles would not have been reversed, for slavinnen did not respond with violence but, rather, with flight), the sentence would have been swift and equally brutal. Oetan, said the aldermen, had "[fallen] into despotism according to the law," and Tjindra was to be sold at public auction "with the interdiction on the defendant against directly or indirectly buying or selling Tjindra and that Tjindra should never again directly or indirectly come under her authority under penalty of confiscation and prosecution."[11] Second (and most profitable for the bench), "the proceeds from the sale of aforementioned Tjindra van Bali shall be declared transferred and confiscated for the needs of the [aldermen]." Finally, Oetan was to be "saddled with all costs and expenses of the Justitie," that is, to pay legal fees and court costs.[12]

Even the lowest class had upper echelons, and when women were violent, the abuse tended to travel a one-way path down the social ladder, descending upon their underlings. With near uniformity, the women who ordered or committed acts of violence were in a position of authority and power over their victims, and those victims were usually bound to their mistresses and masters by purely economic ties. Like most slavinnen, when Tjindra wanted out of her relationship of daily abuse she chose to run away rather than retaliate. Whereas even the least among male slaves was sometimes known to meet fire with fire, slavinnen responded differently. The social construction of a slavin's behavior and identity circumscribed her response to violence such that reciprocating in kind was outside the realm of the possible for the subaltern slavin in Indonesia. If the answer from men who had suffered enough was to fight, women on the edge often chose flight, running away from their master or mistress. In the most extreme cases, the abused sought to take their own life, the ultimate flight.

We must assume that most of the violence and abuse in the city never entered the historical record. It went on behind closed doors and with the quiet consent of friends and neighbors, a societal consensus that discipline in the form of violent punishment was necessary for the perpetuation of a master-slave, mistress-slavin society. There were, however, limits imposed on this "discipline." Occasionally the abuse became so excessive that the state got involved, as it did in Tjindra's case. More commonly, the state stepped in firmly only when a slave retaliated against an abusive mistress or master.

The Widow Maurits and Mono

Mono van Bugis was another slavin victimized by an abusive mistress. The records are not as extensive for Mono as they are for Tjindra, but we still manage to get a good picture of how, when women were abusive they took it out on their underlings, how abuse was more likely when their relationships with their subordinates were economic, and how abused women responded by fleeing, in some instances seeking death. Mono belonged to the Widow Maurits. The widow's last name tells us that she was once married to a man with European status, and her first name, or lack thereof, tells us that the Widow Maurits probably never converted to Christianity, never taking a Christian first name. When Mono testified in July 1765, she did not know how old she was.

The aldermen Jan Breekhout and Jan Hendriz Srerijn thought Mono appeared to be about thirty or thirty-one years old.[13]

The Widow Maurits had her own business (we are not told which kind), probably having inherited a joint estate from her husband and running it independently, as women throughout Southeast Asia frequently did. Mono worked at the warehouse, probably for commercial transshipping, and she was entrusted with the keys to the warehouse. One day, to Mono's horror, her key broke, and she was too scared to tell the Widow Maurits. For three weeks Mono managed to keep the broken key a secret from her mistress. On July 31, Mono decided to put an end to her worries by going and paying to get another key made. Like most slaves and slavinnen, Mono also had an income independent of her mistress and had the financial means to try to bail herself out of her problem.

On her way to get the key made, Mono ran into an unnamed nyai. The nyai kindly "persuaded" Mono to stay with her at the nyai's house until the evening. The nyai was smart enough not to draw attention to herself by entertaining Mono too long. Under Batavian law, keeping a slave or slavin for more than two meals was considered theft and kidnapping. When they reached the Widow Maurits's house, the nyai who had previously been so warm then turned on Mono, however. The nyai lied and told the Widow Maurits that she had caught Mono trying to escape. The widow paid the nyai and immediately put Mono in chains. Mono had been conned by the nyai and was now forced to try and work around the house in chains.[14]

Unhappy with the turn of events, the Widow Maurits began abusing her slavin. Mono says that she was "continually beaten." Things got worse when Mono's food rations were cut in half. The beating had become a ritual in which the Widow Maurits would tie Mono to a makeshift rack, or ladder, and the torture would begin. Finally, relates Mono, "out of desperation" one morning as her mistress was tying her to the ladder, the slavin found a knife and tried to end her own life by stabbing herself in the breast. Bound and unable to bear any more, Mono chose suicide, the only flight path available to her. The very fact that we have Mono's testimony means she was unsuccessful. After the failed suicide attempt, the Widow Maurits must have also found the situation unlivable. She took Mono out of her chains and handed her over to the court to be tried for the property crime of attempted suicide.

Tan Kiok and Ontong

Tan Kiok van Manila was another female superior who "continually" abused her economically tied underling Ontong van Ende, in this case eliciting a gendered response. From her name, we can guess that Tan Kiok was a Chinese mestiza, probably accompanying the Chinese man Que Kienko traveling from the Philippines to the Indies. We must also guess as to her social role within the household. In her own statements, Tan Kiok refers to herself as a "housekeeper," while others (most notably the bailiff David Julius van Aitsma, but also an abused slave under her) refer to her as a concubine.[15] Whether housekeeper or concubine, Tan Kiok was the mistress over the slave Ontong van Ende.[16]

The mistress came downstairs one October morning in 1777 with the house door keys and found the back door open. Since Que Kienko lay sick upstairs, Tan Kiok ran the day-to-day operations in the household.[17] Leaving the door open would probably have been enough to elicit a severe reprimand from most masters or mistresses, but it troubled Tan Kiok particularly because, attached to their house, was a food stall that during the day was looked after by a Chinese helper, Tan Biouko, who also lived with Que Kienko. Ontong cut sugarcane for a living, and he would come home and prepare the cane with the knife in front of the attached food stall. Tan Kiok proceeded to interrogate her slaves and "the boy"; and Ontong van Ende stood accused of leaving the door open by his fellow slaves. As Tan Kiok tells it, when she confronted Ontong, he cursed her and she "had to beat him with a Javanese rattan and he was not pleased." The slave was so displeased in fact that he grabbed the rattan, picked Tan Kiok up into the air, threw her to the ground, and walked out the door. It was noon.

Que Kienko ordered Tan Kiok to call in the kaffirs (the native police) to round up Ontong and bring him back. In his later confession, Ontong recalled the "continual" beatings and said it made him "despondent."[18] Now a fugitive, Ontong evaded the kaffirs, and while Tan Kiok was busy locking up the back door, Ontong crept into the food stall at eight o'clock in the evening, where he "resolved to kill her that night with a sailor's knife." Returning from their search, native police stumbled upon Ontong in the food stall. In the melee, as the kaffirs were trying to try to wrest the knife from the slave's hand, Ontong killed a Chinese named Que Seengko, stabbing him in the left cheek and right underarm.

Ontong's crime would not go unpunished, but Tan Kiok's behavior would not constitute a crime. The lives of Asians living under eighteenth-century Dutch control were dominated for the most part by local Asian custom and practice, but when Asians broke the criminal law superimposed by the Dutch, they were judged by Roman Dutch legal standards. As a civil code, the law was meant to be comprehensive, and rulings were to be based not on common law or other legal or social precedent but on the letter of the law itself. This, however, did not preclude colonial officials from occasionally reaching outside the code and seeking biblical precedent for moral justification in putting a slave to death. Because Ontong had used a knife, the aldermen looked to Numbers 35:16 for an answer, "And if he smite him with an instrument of iron, so that he die, he *is* a murderer: the murderer shall surely be put to death." And since Ontong sought to ambush Tan Kiok, the court cited Deuteronomy 19:11, "If any man hate his neighbor, and lie in wait for him, and rise up against him, and smite him mortally that he die, and fleeth into one of these cities: Then the elders of his city shall send and fetch him thence, and deliver him into the hand of the avenger of blood, that he may die." For most Asians in early modern Batavia, the Dutch functioned as little more than referees, standing on the sidelines of a much larger Asian social system. But when a crime was committed, the distance closed; people were detained, men and women were interrogated, and sentences were carried out. Ontong's penalty was meant both as a punishment to him and as a deterrent to others. He was ordered to be bound face-down to a cross and put to death "without mercy," having his head chopped off with an axe; "thereafter the head is to be put on a stake and the head displayed in plain sight."[19]

Nyai Bintje and Tapasan

In the unique world of Southeast Asian bondage, slaves and slavinnen often had independent incomes, access to credit, and a possibility of buying or inheriting their own freedom. Tapasan van Bali was one such slave. His owners, a "free Balinese man" named Bapak Sabil (*Sabil* means "just" or "holy" in modern Malay/Indonesian) and a "free Balinese woman" named Nyai Bintje, had purchased him for fifty rijksdaalders.[20] Tapasan worked hard to pay off his "coolie loan," the debt of labor owed by a slave to his owner; he had to arrange to purchase his freedom from Sabil and

Bintje for an additional ten rijksdaalders over what they had paid for him (apparently he had been appreciating in value). From Tapasan's testimony, it seems he might have been content to remain a coolie slave but was tired of his master and mistress saying "that regardless of all his labors to please his master and mistress, they physically and verbally abused him daily."[21]

While Tapasan had been working hard to pay his debt, he was also busy negotiating a loan from a creditor on the local market, Intje Pandarongan who lived on the market at Wel te Vreden. According to Tapasan, he had already given Bapak Sabil fifty rijksdaalders of his loan money, and on a March morning in 1778 he asked his master if he could go into town and get the rest to buy his freedom. Sabil ordered Tapasan to get back to work in the "plantation." Although, in Malay, Bapak Sabil's name means "just or holy," Tapasan felt little of these qualities in his owners. Tapasan's freedom would end what had been a very advantageous economic relationship for Bapak Sabil and Nyai Bintje. Tapasan refused to go to work, saying that he needed to go to the market. Sabil ordered again, and Tapasan "wholeheart-edly continued to refuse." Tapasan continued to reason with his master, but Sabil grew tired and began scolding and threatening him. It made him angry, Sabil said, "that his own slave was talking back to him."[22]

Like the many other slaves and slavinnen who claimed to be sinking into a deep despair after "continual beatings" from their superiors, Tapasan "became disconsolate from the daily mistreatment" he endured under his master and mistress, and he "made the decision to seek revenge."[23] Nyai Bintje also concedes that Tapasan was crestfallen, but she claims that she had never abused him, and he was disheartened because he wanted to emancipate himself for thirty or forty rijksdaalders instead of the fifty for which he was purchased.[24] Whether from the beating or from freedom's price tag, when he came to the end of his rope Tapasan responded as male slaves commonly did.

As his master stood screaming at him, Tapasan reached into his waist-band and pulled out an axe blade (in Malay, *tombak*). In terror, Bapak Sabil took off running for the house calling to Bintje for help. Bintje had just woken up and come out of her room when Sabil burst through the door with Tapasan in hot pursuit, stopping only to pick up a piece of wood on the way in. Tapasan broke off the chase with his master and headed straight for his mistress. Tapasan struck Bintje in the head with the piece of wood and slashed her several times with the axe blade.[25] Bintje said that he would have finished her off, but he heard someone coming and ran into the bedroom. Bapak Sabil and several others cornered him in the bedroom, ordering him to put down his weapon. When he refused, his master shot him in the left arm, which later had to be amputated.[26] Tapasan was sentenced to death.[27] This was a guaranteed fate for any slave or slavin who assaulted their master.

Kiauwa and Laka

On the whole, the lowest echelons of the female underclass were much less likely than their male counterparts to retaliate with violence when subjected to repeated physical abuse from a brutal mistress, master, or other social superior. Most male slaves on the edge fought back at their abusive overlords. One, however, opted for suicide as the way out of a violent household.

Depending on who was telling the story, Kiauwa van Passier was either the slavin or the concubine of the Chinese man Tan Koko. According to Tan Koko's slave Laka van Timor, Kiauwa was a concubine who "continually" beat Laka, and when he complained to his master about her, Tan Koko defended her and instead blamed the slave. For this reason, Laka petitioned his master to be sold, but Tan Koko would "lend no ear." Laka said he felt "disheartened" and went and gambled away all of his own clothes. Then, as Laka remembered it, one Saturday afternoon in March 1777 as he sat in front of his master's house playing a mouth harp he had just purchased, Kiauwa the concubine came over to take the harp away from him, saying it was hers.[28] When Laka refused to give it to her, Kiauwa beat him in the face with a Chinese pipe, giving Laka a bloody nose.[29]

Kiauwa remembers the encounter somewhat differently. First of all she describes herself as "a slavin of the Chinese Tan Koko," not a concubine. In the slippage between what defined a slavin and a concubine, it seems that Kiauwa chose to exonerate herself by self-identifying as a slavin with stewardship over none, for as the court repeatedly experienced, female slaves of that station did not resort to vengeful violence. Kiauwa (now the lowly slavin) recalls Laka coming into the house one afternoon wearing an old shirt and a scarf on his head. According to Kiauwa's deposition given

8 April 1777, Laka did not answer when master Tan asked Laka where his shirt and other things were, and Kiauwa turned to her master, saying "I have seen him for days now walking around without a good shirt or scarf on."[30] Then, Kiauwa concludes, she left and returned to her sewing. As was customary, three days after that initial statement, Kiauwa returned to confirm her testimony and to expressly deny having hit Laka with a Chinese pipe, signing her deposition with what appears to be a rough Chinese character.[31] Perhaps Tan Koko had been training her to run his business.

Did she indeed abuse him? That much is unclear. What is certain is that things escalated between master and slave, and Tan Koko proceeded to beat Laka (one witness said with a chain) demanding an answer about Laka's missing clothing. Eventually, Laka confessed that he had gambled his scarf, shirt (*badje*, in Malay *baju*), and sarong away, the beating stopped, and Laka went back into the house. Sinking further into the sadness allegedly prompted by Kiauwa's incessant beatings, Laka retired to the back of the house where he said he "fell into temptation," resolving to take his own life. Kiauwa heard another of Tan Koko's slaves, Laijkoeij van Siam (a Thai slave), cry out that Laka had taken a little knife out of his own pants pocket and was holed up inside a back room. When they approached him, Laka attempted suicide by cutting himself in the throat but "with truly no intention of harming anyone else."[32]

Again, extreme and "incessant" abuse elicited an extreme response from a coolie. Fortunately for his master and mistress, Laka did not seek the path most traveled by other men but chose suicide over murder. Murder or attempted murder would have certainly bought Laka the death penalty but his attempted suicide, like that of the slavin Mono van Bugis, was also considered a serious offence. The Court of Aldermen took an interest in Laka because "the slave thereby attempted to rob his master of the slave's body and through a murder-execution to help himself out of this world." He was sentenced to be bound to a pole, beaten severely on the bare back with rods (presumably rattan), branded, chained, sent to labor for ten years on the public works, thereafter banned, and saddled with court costs.[33] Opting for suicide over murder, Laka demonstrated that although men and women of that station tended toward differing responses to violence, the delimitations were not absolute, and the sins of a slave or—as we shall see—a slavin occasionally transgressed those boundaries.

Soliang and Sinliang

Sinliang van Bali had "borne the yoke of slavery," as the state put it, for a little over a month when she pulled a knife out of her blouse and delivered a small puncture wound to the chest of her master, Oeij Tjungko.[34] Nyai Mensing, Oeij's concubine and mother to his suckling child, had recently passed away. Nursing a baby of her own, Sinliang van Bali had been purchased by Oeij to nurse his motherless child. This was Sinliang's first experience as a slavin, and we can only guess as to the circumstances that brought her to this "unhappy state of slavery wherein she [found] herself."[35] Perhaps she had been the unfortunate victim of a slave raid. Since the mid-seventeenth century, most of Batavia's slaves came from the Indonesian archipelago, especially eastern Indonesia, instead of Bengal or other mainland Asian ports. With her small child still by her side, though, a more likely scenario was that she entered into bondage to pay an even more unbearable debt, not unlike Nyo Kinnio who sold herself into concubinage to the man who paid for the burial of her father.

Sinliang's duties were not limited to wet-nursing. A week before the attack on Oeij, his servants were forced to come and fish her out, when, while fetching water to wash the rice, she had fallen into a well (not an inappropriate metaphor for her new social status within the household).[36] Oeij's household consisted of at least one slave named Si Oralia van Bali and three "freed slavinnen," Soliang van Timor, Macier, and Mauwar van Sumbauwa who had also wet-nursed the deceased Nyai Mensing's child.[37] Their opinion of Sinliang was not high, and several references are made to her stupidity and lack of focus. Days before the stabbing on 26 November 1792, Soliang, the Timorese slavin, "hit [Sinliang] because she was not paying attention."[38] Sinliang was newly initiated into slavery and immediately stuck on the bottom rung of the household hierarchy. The breaking point for this slavin could not have been great.

At four in the afternoon of the day in question, Sinliang came to the freed slavin Mauwar complaining of stomach pain. The woman, who had also wet-nursed Oeij's baby, rubbed several medicines on Sinliang's stomach and stayed with her and the children. We do not know if the beating Sinliang received from the freed slavin Soliang caused her stomachache, but it seems likely, since after about an hour with Mauwar, Sinliang arose, "upset from the blows she had received," and took a knife out from underneath Soliang's mat.[39] Oeij saw Sinliang doubled over and, as he later described, "acting as though her body was in pain," and he went to help upright her. When he did, she pulled the knife out from underneath her blouse and struck Oeij in the right breast. Two hours later, reported surgeon J. de Raath, Oeij Tjunkgo only had "a little swelling," but at the time of the incident Oeij said it was enough to send him into shock, such that he was "unable to defend himself and simply held her off his body with both hands while calling for help." Sioralia van Bali heard "the cry of 'Amok!'" and subdued Sinliang.[40]

It was not until the next day, 27 November 1792, that Oeij brought in his "property," the slavin Sinliang van Bali, and handed her over to the law. Oeij did not speak Malay and had the Chinese Lim Tjouwsung translate for him.[41] When, after an uncharacteristically long wait, the aldermen gathered statements around the end of December, the court was getting nowhere, so they brought everyone together again in early February. Why all the trouble? "The investigation could not proceed as it should," said lead prosecutor Steven Poelman, because they had been receiving "confusing and contradictory statements from the witnesses and the imprisoned slavin." Poelman had "a superficial confession" from Sinliang of "lightly assault[ing] her master," an offense punishable by death, but there was dispute as to Sinliang's diminished capacity.[42]

The court was at an impasse because of two specific issues. First, after only a month of slavery, was Sinliang "sorely grieved" by the gulf between her "former freedom and the unhappy state of slavery," including Soliang's abuse, and too "humiliated" by "no longer being in control over the mother's milk of her own body, but forced instead to give it to a strange child"? The court asked, "Was this not all sufficient to magnify her sadness and despair over being the wet-nurse for her master's child in addition to enduring beatings from another who, by her [Sinliang's] understanding should have no authority or power to do so"? Amazingly, the prosecutor began to advocate Sinliang's position. Under Roman Dutch law, the defendant was not represented by independent counsel in a criminal proceeding. Theoretically, the trained jurists of the court neutrally weighed the merits of a given case, passing impartial judgment. In reality the defendant was presumed guilty by virtue of his or her arrest, and most of the legal wrangling went on over the sentencing. Poelman asked if another mother would not have done the same in Sinliang's position, and the aldermen wondered if Sinliang had really been able to internalize her new role as a slavin? If so would she have done what she did?

A second problem debated by the court was Sinliang's mental state. Again, it had her confession, but by 8 April 1793 the aldermen were of the increasing opinion that "such a confession [was] in no way full." In their view, Sinliang had merely snapped because of the shock of her new slavin status, adding "clearly no evil will or bad intentions shine through in her confession, only a dimness of faculties and a lack of natural acumen to be able to comprehend the weighty consequences of such actions." Not only was Sinliang physically ill, recorded court clerk Pieter Jan du Bois, but the aldermen Christiaan Louis Arnold and Johannes van Hek commented on her "persistent and considerable stupidity and limited intellect." There were serious questions about Sinliang's ability to discern right from wrong. Whether real or imagined, these questions saved Sinliang from the executioner—but not from a heavy sentence. She was condemned to labor for life in chains on the public works in the Ambachtsquartier (Craftsmen's Quarter).[43] It was a lighter sentence, but the gallows might have been more merciful. Given Batavia's already legendary insalubrity, it is difficult to imagine a slavin on rations surviving long while dredging the filth from the city canals or performing any other of the many onerous tasks for convicted felons. For this reason, Sinliang's sentence was in effect a death sentence, just more drawn out.

Sinliang van Bali, the slavin lowest in the pecking order, took a knife and stabbed her master in the chest. When a male slave committed a similar crime, even while claiming to have lost touch with reality, his plea of "amok" was dismissed out of hand and he was executed "swiftly" and "without mercy." Because violent behavior from slavinnen without gainful underlings was simply beyond the pale, the court constructed Sinliang not as a slavin but as a feeble-minded nursing mother who had not yet assumed the lowly mantle of slavin. Batavia could govern this kind of woman. But nothing was more frightening and hence more unimaginable than a population of underclass women who would rise up and smite their masters.

Hang Kienio and Tjambang

If violence traveled down the social ladder, there were often several degrees of separation between a woman perched upon its top rung and the slave she ordered beaten by one of her minions, but this gap between mistress and slave could be bridged in an instant when he retaliated, going straight for the higher source of his suffering. Hang Kienio remembered sitting at home chatting with her female friends one evening in 1783. Kienio had been married to the captain of the Chinese nation Ong Tjoeseeng. As in many Southeast Asian maritime entrepots, the various ethnic groups were divided into "nations," and civic administration was divided up among the so-called captains who stood at the head of each nation. At his passing, Captain Ong Tjoeseeng had left Hang Kienio in command of a sizeable estate, including a household with no fewer than eleven slaves, slavinnen, and attendants. It was around seven in that September night when a Makassarese slave named Tjambang came strolling in with no pants on but wearing only a *kancut* or short loin cloth. Hang Kienio found it "incredibly ill-mannered" for him to be so underdressed in front of the other women and called in two members of her household, Letjong van Sumbauwa and Intje Soekoer, "to forcefully break him of this impertinent habit by giving him a few swats with a rattan cane."[44]

Letjong van Sumbauwa was Hang Kienio's coachman, and a freed slave according to the law, though this did not preclude Kienio from constantly referring to Letjong as just a slave.[45] Having a coachman means having a carriage, another clue as to Hang Kienio's relative affluence and importance. Dutch officials in Batavia had adopted Asian symbols of wealth and status (including riding in the grand procession, borne aloft and shaded by umbrellas, with slave entourage); the statutes of Batavia included law codes meant to limit the use of coach riding and parasol sporting to the elite.[46] Hang Kienio charged Letjong the coachman and the mandor Injte Soekoer with the task of punishing Tjambang.

They brought the pantless slave outside in front of the house, and Letjong held him down while Intje Soekoer delivered three blows to the small of the back with the rattan. "At the moment when I began to be beaten," described Tjambang, "my eyes went dark," and he retreated into his hut as soon as it was over.[47] In the criminal proceedings, many slaves related how in these moments of great tension, a darkness descended over them and they lost all capacity for self-control. According to several eyewitness accounts (from Intje Soekoer, a mandor; Letjong van Sumbauwa, the coachman; and one Slammat van Makassar), Tjambang then produced a knife and came after Hang Kienio. Caught in his path was a fellow slave named Pondok van Bugis. Tjambang stabbed him in the chest, and Pondok fled screaming "he's running amok!"[48]

Pandemonium broke out at Kienio's, and the household scurried in panic. Despite his blind rage, Tjambang locked in on his target and stormed the house heading straight for Hang Kienio. Another bystander was caught in the doorway between Tjambang and Hang Kienio. Kienio's slavin, Tata van Makassar, missed the caning because she had been bringing rice to the "house folk." (It is unclear whether Tata included herself under that umbrella or whether she considered herself an agricultural coolie slavin who worked in the fields to bring home the rice.) In any case, her return was poorly timed, for when she turned to enter the house, she was knocked over with a "push from behind." Testifying in bandages from the city surgeon's, Tata did not know that she had been injured until she felt "the warmth of the blood gushing from her wound." Standing up, she turned and again met Tjambang's blade, which added an inch-long gash in her right shoulder bone and another in her right arm to the initial puncture wound in the left gluteus maximus, according to the surgeon.[49]

Finally Tjambang stood face-to-face with his mistress. For him there had been no doubt as to the source of his suffering. He swung the knife at her heart, only to have it bounce off her chest. Again he struck and again the knife would not penetrate. Miraculously, the knife twice ricocheted off the medallion she wore; she had been saved by her own ostentatious display of wealth.[50] A third blow, however, penetrated the left side of her stomach, and Hang Kienio fell to the ground where she was "nearly trampled by the fleeing crowd." Someone pulled her to safety, but not before Tjambang wounded her again, this time in the left arm. Mission accomplished, Tjambang bolted for the *Herenweg* but was struck down and disarmed by the slave Slammat van Makassar, who happened to be nearby carrying water.

Hang Keinio was a powerful woman with important family connections. Her deceased husband was captain of the Chinese nation, and her nephew Gouw Tjansie was the lieutenant of the Chinese nation. Gouw Tjansie came immediately upon hearing the news of the attack at his aunt's house. Another of her nephews, Ong Tjoebeeng, lived with Hang Keinio, and he and Gouw Tjansie detained Tjambang and a slave named Lijoe van Makassar until the authorities arrived. Tjansie testified that Lijoe had been "an eyewitness yet did not pursue or attempt to subdue Tjambang."[51] Lijoe could not remain an innocent bystander while his mistress was being attacked (an early modern "Good Samaritan" law). In addition, the live-in nephew Ong Tjoebeeng (also called Ruen Tjoebang) swore that he heard Tjambang, while he was bound, say to Lijoe, "What are you saying? Are you deceiving me or do you not keep your word?" painting Lijoe as some kind of accomplice.

In her statement of 18 September 1793, Hang Kienio said that her husband had bought Lijoe seven years before when the slave was still "green," meaning presumably that Hang Kienio's household was Lijoe's first experience as a slave. Some of her slaves and slavinnen did domestic labor, but many worked on Hang Kienio's sugar plantation and sugar mill. Lijoe had been purchased together with eleven other slaves (including Tjambang) by her deceased husband. Many Batavian crimes, especially theft and escape, were seen as conspiracies by slaves who had served or were serving together under a common master or mistress; though still under Hang Kienio, Lijoe had been laboring in the sugar mill for several months prior to being summoned to the house.

The day after the incident Tjambang, Lijoe, and the others were brought to testify at city hall. From the beginning Lijoe maintained his innocence, and Tjambang pleaded "amok." Tjambang was indicted on the ironic charge of "willful assault by amok."[52] If genuine, amok was by its very nature not willful, but the court was apparently growing impatient with an increase in the number of "terrible and detestable crime[s]" blamed on amok, "known all too well here locally."[53] Despite Tjambang's description of darkness descending over his eyes, the aldermen were convinced that he had planned the attack.

Tjambang, whom the court clerk at trial described as "apprehended as he now stands, with a short garment about his body, without pants," stated that he "normally walked around without pants" and "was apprehended and beaten with a rattan without having done anything wrong." According to Tjambang, he came home that night after drinking two *duit* worth of arrack (palm wine) and was being falsely accused because he was "naive." This was unsatisfactory for the gentlemen aldermen. They had witnesses and a rich and angry mistress; the aldermen wanted a confession, and they needed a confession to be able to issue the death sentence they knew awaited Tjambang for stabbing his mistress. One of Hang Kienio's domestic *slavinnen*, Tjong Kuee van Bali who worked in the cooking shed attached to the outside of the house, reported that one of her knives had been missing, and she swore that Tjambang "had long been filled/consumed with the disastrous intention of committing a blood bath."[54] A few weeks later, Tjambang was brought back and given a "sharp examination"—meaning he was tortured so that he might confess. Still unrelenting, Tjambang was tortured twice on 2 November 1793 to answer a list of questions spanning twenty pages. Much of the questioning focused on where he obtained the knife ("From a *clontong* Chinese for nine stivers," he said) and which of his fellow slaves had knives. Under torture he gave the revised version of what transpired that night:

> I took out the blade from under my pillow and, keeping it with me because I was going out to drink arrack and it was quite common for me to be armed with a knife. I came home and walked around by the kitchen with my garment and came face-to-face with my mistress who had no other women with her. For this I got a beating.[55]

He confessed to the assault charges and was sentenced to have his right hand cut off, to be bound to a cross and decapitated; his head, body, and hand would be put on display and left "as prey to the birds." He was also fined for court costs. Lijoe dodged the reaper, was sentenced to a flogging, and was turned over to Hang Kienio to work off the court costs that his mistress had to pay up front for him.[56]

*H*ang Kienio and the cases of women like her are significant as they exhibit similar tendencies among the different cases of female violence in Batavia. Violence, when it occurred, crept down the social ladder. As a rule, these victims did not live inside but outside the mistresses' families and were viewed as something akin to draft animals. In each case the incident that precipitated the criminal act (thus involving the court and the historian) was not the first such instance of abuse but seemed to the victim to be over the top or the drop that spilled the bucket. Intriguingly, the sexes sought distinctly different solutions to their unbearable burden: men chose to fight and women chose to run.

Another important way in which the stories of the women of Batavia are important is that they portend consequential but often unseen changes on the historical horizon. As plantations radiated outward from late eighteenth-century Batavia, there became less space for the "cozy" intimacy of pure household slavery. Slaves and slavinnen who might have been absorbed into the lower rungs of their master's or mistress's extended family or who might have been kept on in the household as part of a prestige entourage were being recast as financial investments for which their owners expected a financial return.

Just a few decades later (1830 and beyond) when the colonial bottom line no longer centered around the scarcity-driven, restrictive monopoly system, the Indonesian underclass would pay a dear price on the free market. In the belly of the nineteenth-century global market rumbled an insatiable appetite for mass quantities of coffee, indigo, sugar, tea, and tobacco, for which international demand seemed limitless and supplies were never enough. The late modern Dutch colonial state imagined, for the first time, that all Indonesians fell under its umbrella and began viewing the masses as economic entities. The same pragmatism that drove earlier generations of Dutch into a limited embrace with a few Asians and out of the lives of the vast majority now called for the reorientation of the entire economy. Beginning with the Cultivation System in 1830, the colonial economy centered around cash cropping and demanded one-fifth of the already meager local output, even at the cost of widespread famine and disruption.

Conclusion

The eighteenth century saw a change in the nature of relationships of dependency in the colonies of Dutch Asia. Masters and mistresses began calculating the value of their underlings less in terms of the return in prestige or status derived from an urban entourage and more in terms of the economic return provided by a plantation labor force. The first laws promulgated by the VOC advanced the Company's position that slaves were economic units or property and established a clear distinction between slaves and free persons. The results were mixed. Many slaves, even abetted by their owners, functioned as free persons until their exploits put them on the aldermen's radar. Other slaves' masters and mistresses, however, internalized the state's understanding of slavery. Their mistreatment of their slaves, in terms of physical abuse or in terms of hindering social advancement, could bring their relationships with their slaves to a point of confrontation where the law became involved and a criminal case ensued.

Still, the demographic underpinnings and economic foundations of the colonial relationship remained constant well into the nineteenth century. Change, however, was on the horizon. Many of the underclass were caught in the late eighteenth-century advance in the wheels of commerce. The VOC enjoyed huge profits through most of the 1600s, but at the very moment that the VOC's stranglehold on spices was absolute, in the last quarter of the seventeenth century, European demand began to shift away from the fine spices, and trade volume shifted to textiles, coffee, and tea, over which the VOC did not and could not ever have a monopoly. Some things even the Company could not control. To try to compensate for the losses, an increasing percentage of VOC revenues after 1690 came from tolls, taxes, and tributes collected through an expanding colonial administration that ruled over ever-increasing territorial holdings in Africa and Asia.

Overhead costs more than kept pace with Company growth throughout the eighteenth century until, crippled by debts of almost 100 million guilders and reeling from the fourth Anglo-Dutch war and the French control over the Netherlands beginning in 1795, the VOC dissolved on December 31, 1799. Called "a curious and indecisive transition period between these two great ages," the late eighteenth century is a pivotal moment in Indonesian and Southeast Asian history.[1] From this time, Dutch colonial authority began slowly to span the entire Indonesian archipelago and to reach into the daily lives of its disparate nations and peoples. Only then can we speak of the "Dutch period" of Indonesian history and the predominance of the plantation economy. After 1800 the Dutch squeezed the East Indies harder in order to compensate for lagging state revenues in the Netherlands, first using native elite to force Javanese peasants to deliver coffee, indigo, sugar, tea, and tobacco to the Dutch from 1830 to 1870 (the Cultivation System), then opening the archipelago to large-scale private capital investment after 1870 (the Liberal Period), and finally promising though never delivering widespread reform from 1900 onward (the Ethical Period).[2]

Before 1800 the Company's modus operandi was to exercise total control over a smaller number of sites such as Makassar, Batavia, Ambon, and Melaka, which meant establishing and running the local judicial system. Only tiny toeholds in the vast Indonesian archipelago (also known as the East Indies) could truly be considered the "Dutch" East Indies until the nineteenth century. The present and (barely) unitary state of the Republic of Indonesia is a colonial construct that only gradually began to be assembled by the late modern colonial state, and it was only in place for a few decades before World War II. But even after the East Indies and the Dutch East Indies became synonymous in the early twentieth century, administrators from other European colonial powers marveled at Dutch indirect rule. That the Dutch colonial state had managed to do so much with so little direct administration encouraged others to study the model so they "might learn much where the Dutch may seem to have succeeded."[3] Previous Dutch colonial presence in the archipelago was even more "indirect" than its late modern incarnation. However, in those few early modern locales in which the Dutch East India Company was the actual governing authority, Dutch rule was direct and Dutch colonial law was the ruling standard for European and Asian alike.

In the VOC period, as long as advantageous trade relationships abounded, the Company preferred to work out extraterritoriality arrangements for its own employees and otherwise cut costs by letting indigenous law prevail throughout the rest of the archipelago and beyond. These were not the only options for early modern Dutch influence, however. Mason Hoadley, in his book *Selective Judicial Competence*, details an example of VOC intervention in Javanese legal procedure in the Prianger regency, a type of intervention that became more frequent in the succeeding colonial era.[4] Rather than bearing the financial burden of manning their own courts, the Company exercised "selective judicial competence," for example, excluding Islamic scholars from subjects' (*padu*) court and adding a royal appointee (*jaksa*) on that same body. Hoadley's explanation of selective VOC intervention fits well with much of what we know about that organization: it was a pragmatic response to local circumstance, based on maximum return for minimum investment.

With the death of the Company and the rise of a new colonial economy, beginning with the expansion of the plantation complex in the eighteenth century and culminating in the Cultivation System of 1830, the Dutch colonial state needed a more elaborate legal and racial hierarchy to articulate "essential" differences between native and European. Out of this impulse evolved the study of native customary law or adat. In the colonies, twentieth-century jurists and anthropologists collaborated to produce bundles of *adatrecht*, which set in stone what had previously been dynamic and constantly evolving systems of customary law. As a result, Europeans (and the tiny handful of Asians considered part of the civil registry [*burgerlijke stand*]) were governed by one juridical order while the rest of Indonesia lived under the several *Inlandsch Reglement* (Native Regulations) and the many adat law bundles. The more unitary the colonial state became, the more plural the legal order it employed. When it happened, the Ethici argued that the codification and implementation of customary law would spare the Indonesian masses from the culturally blind and insensitive

European law and shelter them from the ravages of naked capitalism.[5] But as Dan Lev has pointed out, "the notion of 'different people, different needs'" also ensured the existence of an exploitable agrarian base, having no recourse to the rights of European law.[6]

When, in the early colonial period, most VOC employees were living with or married to Asian women, it made perfect sense for the Company to treat its employees' spouses as Dutch women. It was also natural for the Dutch to consider all other Asian and Europeans under its control as equals under the law. The absence of European women and the frailty of European men created a pattern of racial mixing and remarriage in which the Asian wives and serial widows of Company men were given not only Dutch legal status but special legal privileges. Regardless of employment status, the colonial law code applied universally, Asians receiving the same treatment as Europeans. This was only feasible given the nature of spice-based economic extraction. Beginning in the nineteenth century, however, the fundamentals of colonial economics would change. Structural changes in the form of the Suez Canal, mosquito eradication, and European female immigration resulted in the reconfiguring of the demographic and social landscape of the Indies. When these foundations of the colonial legal system changed, so too would the legal system itself and with it the very nature of colonialism.

INTRODUCTION

1. "Verklaring van des stads chirurgijn David Beijlon rakende de mishandelinge van de slavinne Tjindra van Balie. no. 3 [25 April 1775]," Algemeen Rijksarchief (General State Archives, The Hague; hereafter cited as ARA), Toegangsnummer (access number) 1.04.18.03, Inventarisnummer (inventory number) 11963. Brackets in the following notes can either connote the addition of a date or information not included in the title of a document or contain the abbreviation of a document previously cited in full. Unless otherwise noted, all translations are my own.

2. "Peranakan," in Declaratoir van Oetan parnakan chinese vrouw voor den heer landdrost Jan Hendrik Poock ratt off. no. 4 [22 May 1775], ARA 1.04.18.03, inv. 11963.

1—GENDER, BONDAGE, AND THE LAW IN EARLY DUTCH ASIA

1. The early Dutch terms *slavin* (singular) and *slavinnen* (plural) refer to female slaves. Especially in Southeast Asia the default category for slave should not automatically be construed as male. Furthermore, the gendered behavior of male and female slaves requires more specificity than is provided in the generic term "slave."

2. F. C. de Haan, *Oud Batavia* (Batavia: G. Kolff, 1922), 451.

3. Ibid., 465–66. Slavery no longer formally existed when de Haan lived and worked in Batavia, but the phenomenon of the native hand rocking the European cradle (along with "wheedling" and "soft tones") was widespread and not altogether welcome.

4. Ibid., 466. Twentieth-century Indonesian author Pramoedya Ananta Toer and Dutch author Louis Couperus both paint vivid pictures of strong women in their period novels.

5. Ibid., 111.

6. Jean Gelman Taylor, *The Social World of Batavia: European and Eurasian in Dutch Asia* (Madison: University of Wisconsin Press, 1983), 39.

7. Leonard Blussé, *Strange Company: Chinese Settlers, Mestizo Women, and the Dutch in VOC Batavia* (Dordrecht: Foris, 1986); Remco Raben, "Batavia and Colombo: The Ethnic and Spatial Order of Two Colonial Cities, 1600–1800"

(dissertation, Rijksuniversiteit Leiden, 1996); Henk Niemeijer's, *Calvinisme en koloniale stadscultuur Batavia, 1619–1725* (Almelo, Netherlands: Biester and Abbes, 1996); Susan Abeyasekere, *Jakarta: A History* (Singapore: Oxford University Press, 1989).

8. Gerritt J. Knaap, "Pants, Skirts, and Pulpits: Women and Gender in Seventeenth-Century Amboina," in Barbara Watson Andaya, ed., *Other Pasts: Women, Gender and History in Early Modern Southeast Asia* (Honolulu: Center for Southeast Asian Studies, University of Hawaii, Manoa, 2000), 147–73; Dhiravat na Pombejra, "VOC Employees and Their Relationships with Mon and Siamese Women: A Case Study of Osoet Pegua," ibid., 195–214; Hendrik E. Niemeijer, "Slavery, Ethnicity and the Economic Independence of Women in Seventeenth-Century Batavia," ibid., 174–94.

9. Niemeijer, "Slavery, Ethnicity and the Economic Independence of Women," ibid., 174. Another important work by one of the field's foremost scholars is Barbara Watson Andaya, "From Temporary Wife to Prostitute: Sexuality and Economic Change in Early Modern Southeast Asia," *Journal of Women's History* 9, no. 4 (1998): 11–34.

10. Frances Gouda contributes to this subject in thoughtful pieces ranging from notions of colonial domesticity, to educating Indonesian girls, to colonial sexuality. See Julia Clancy-Smith and Frances Gouda, eds., *Domesticating the Empire: Race, Gender, and Family Life in French and Dutch Colonialism* (Charlottesville: University Press of Virginia, 1998), and Frances Gouda, *Dutch Culture Overseas: Colonial Practice in the Netherlands Indies, 1900–1942* (Amsterdam: Amsterdam University Press, 1995). See also Reijs Jeske, ed., *Vrouwen in de Nederlandse Kolonien* (Nijmegen: SUN, 1986); Elsbeth Locher-Scholten, *Women and the Colonial State: Essays on Gender and Modernity in the Netherlands Indies, 1900–1942* (Amsterdam: Amsterdam University Press, 2000); Alisa Zainu'ddin, ed., *Kartini Centenary: Indonesian Women Then and Now* (Clayton, Victoria: Centre for Southeast Asian Studies, Monash University, 1980); Ann Stoler, *Carnal Knowledge and Imperial Power: Race and the Intimate in Colonial Rule* (Berkeley and Los Angeles: University of California Press, 2002).

11. Sita van Bemmelen, Madelon Djajadingrat-Niewenhuis, Elsbeth Locher-Scholten, and Elly Touwen-Bouwsma, eds., *Women and Mediation in Indonesia* (Leiden: KITLV Press, 1992); Ester Boserup, *Women's Role in Economic Development* (New York: St. Martin's Press, 1970); Elsbeth Locher-Scholten and Anke Niehof, eds., *Indonesian Women in Focus: Past and Present Notions* (Dordrecht: Foris, 1987); Aihwa Ong and Michael G. Peletz, eds., *Bewitching Women, Pious Men: Gender and Body Politics in Southeast Asia* (Berkeley and Los Angeles: University of California Press, 1995); Barbara N. Ramusack and Sharon Sievers, *Women in Asia* (Bloomington: Indiana University Press, 1999); Laurie J. Sears, ed., *Fantasizing the Feminine in Indonesia* (Durham: Duke University Press, 1996); Maila Stevens, ed., *Why Gender Matters in Southeast Asian Politics*

(Clayton, Victoria: Monash University Southeast Asia Centre, Monash Papers on Southeast Asia no. 41, 1991).

12. James C. Scott, *The Moral Economy of the Peasant: Rebellion and Subsistence in Southeast Asia* (New Haven: Yale University Press, 1976); Clifford Geertz, *Agricultural Involution: The Processes of Ecological Change in Indonesia* (Berkeley and Los Angeles: University of California Press, 1963).

13. Stoler, *Carnal Knowledge*, 22 (quote), 10.

14. Ibid., 22.

15. Fernand Braudel, *The Structures of Everyday Life: The Limits of the Possible* (New York: Perennial Library, 1981), 561.

16. Stoler, *Carnal Knowledge*, 23.

17. John R. W. Smail, "On the Possibility of an Autonomous History of South-East Asia," *Journal of Southeast Asian History* 2, no. 2 (July 1961): 73–105. See also Jacob Cornelius van Leur, *Indonesian Trade and Society: Essays in Asian Social and Economic History* (The Hague: W. van Hoeve, 1967).

18. Anthony Reid, *The Lands below the Winds,* volume 1 of *Southeast Asia in the Age of Commerce* (New Haven: Yale University Press, 1988), 163.

19. Ramusack and Sievers, *Women in Asia*, 89.

20. Sir Thomas Stamford Raffles, *The History of Java* (London: John Murray, 1830), 1:353.

21. Reid, *Lands below the Winds,* 171–72.

22. Ibid., 171.

23. Barbara Watson Andaya, "The Changing Religious Role of Women in Premodern South East Asia," *South East Asia Research* 2, no. 2 (September 1994): 100.

24. See the four volumes of the recent series "Restoring Women to History," ed. Cheryl Johnson-Odim and Margaret Strobel, which includes *Women in Asia*, by Barbara N. Ramusack and Sharon Sievers; *Women in Latin America and the Caribbean*, by Marysa Navarro and Virginia Sanchez Korrol; *Women in the Middle East and North Africa*, by Guity Nashat and Judith E. Tucker; and *Women in Sub-Saharan Africa*, by Iris Berger and E. Frances White.

25. Andaya, "Changing Religious Role of Women," 103, 105–6.

26. Ruth McVey, "Change and Continuity in Southeast Asian Studies," *Journal of Southeast Asian Studies* 26, no. 1 (March 1995): 5.

27. Andaya, *Other Pasts*, 2; Andaya, *Flaming Womb*, chapter 2.

28. Ibid., 5.

29. Ibid., 7.

30. Barbara Watson Andaya, *The Flaming Womb: Repositioning Women in Early Modern Southeast Asia* (Honolulu: University of Hawaii Press, 2006), 49.

31. Locher-Scholten and Niehof, *Indonesian Women in Focus* (Dordrecht: Foris, 1987), 3.

32. Peter Carey and Vincent Houben, "Spirited Srikandhis and Sly Sumbadras: The Social, Political and Economic Role of Women at the Central

Javanese Courts in the Eighteenth and Early Nineteenth Centuries," in ibid., 12.

33. This archival summary also appears in a tract I co-authored for the TANAP program of Leiden University and the National State Archives.

34. Blussé, Niemeijer, and Raben, for example, have been successful in capturing the local flavor in Dutch Asia because their work employs a combination of Company and municipal archives.

35. Sartono Kartodirdjo, *Indonesian Historiography* (Yogyakarta: Kanisius, 2001), 35.

36. They are overlooked not only in publications but in the archives as well. With nearly every record bundle I opened, the original black sand used to dry the ink in Batavia fell from the pages and filled my book tray.

37. Edward Muir and Guido Ruggiero, eds., *History from Crime* (Baltimore: Johns Hopkins University Press, 1994), viii.

38. James C. Scott, *Domination and the Arts of Resistance: Hidden Transcripts* (New Haven: Yale University Press, 1990).

39. Carlo Ginzburg, *The Night Battles: Witchcraft and Agrarian Cults in the Sixteenth and Seventeenth Centuries* (Baltimore: Johns Hopkins University Press, 1992). *The Cheese and the Worms* and *Clues, Myths, and the Historical Method* are related works also by Ginzburg.

40. Ginzburg, *The Night Battles*, xviii, xvii.

41. Emmanuel LeRoy Ladurie, *Montaillou: Cathars and Catholics in a French Village, 1294–1324* (London: Scholar Press, 1978). Ginzburg began writing about the night battling–*benandanti* in the 1960s.

42. Natalie Zemon Davis, *Fictions in the Archives: Pardon Tales and Their Tellers in Sixteenth-Century France* (Stanford: Stanford University Press, 1987). Davis's *The Return of Martin Guerre* is her most well-recognized study in truth, law, and history.

43. Sometimes, literate witnesses delivered their own written testimony (in Arabic, Chinese, or Javanese, for example), to which the court attached a notarized translation.

44. Fernand Braudel, *Civilization and Capitalism, 15th–18th Century: The Structures of Everyday Life* (Berkeley and Los Angeles: University of California Press, 1992), 29.

2—ASIA TRADE AND LIMITS OF THE POSSIBLE

1. For more on this phenomenon, see Taylor, *The Social World of Batavia*; Blussé, *Strange Company*; and Leonard Blussé, *Bitters Bruid: Een Koloniaal Huwelijksdrama in de Gouden Eeuw* (Amersfoort: Balans, 1997).

2. Jayakarta has since been shortened to Jakarta.

3. Captain Cooke counted no more than twenty European women on his late-eighteenth-century visit to Batavia. De Haan, *Oud Batavia*, 541.

4. The Khoi Khoi are an indigenous ethnic group spanning Southern Africa and were primarily a pastoral people when the VOC arrived in the seventeenth century.

5. J. R. Bruijn, F. S. Gaastra, and I. Schöffer, *Dutch-Asiatic Shipping in the Seventeenth and Eighteenth Centuries* (The Hague: Martinus Nijhoff, 1987), 170. The actual numbers for 1602–1795 are 973,000 departing voyagers from Europe; 802,400 arrivals in Asia; 367,300 departing voyagers from Asia; 322,500 arrivals in Europe.

6. European newcomers were as ill-equipped for tropical disease as Amerindians were for European pathogens.

7. P. H. van der Brug, *Malaria en Malaise: De VOC in Batavia in de achttiende eeuw* (Amsterdam: De Bataafsche Leeuw, 1994), is a careful and groundbreaking study on disease in the Company period.

8. For its young to multiply, *anopheles sundiacus* needs still-standing brackish water. In Batavia, disease raged in the dry month of August and the wet month of January. Dry August conditions allowed the mosquito larvae to hatch unmolested by driving rain; the driving rains of January decreased the salinity of the water, which increased the vegetation in the pond, which then protected the larvae.

9. Raffles's physician and others noticed that the Batavians who slept in raised houses or on the upper floors were much healthier, though it was not then apparent why.

10. The effect that the various diseases had on cultural contacts between Europeans and non-Europeans in the Atlantic and between Europeans and non-Europeans in Asia is markedly different. Throughout the Amerindian populations of the Americas, new European diseases—most notably smallpox—exterminated entire civilizations.

11. Regarding sixteenth-century Sao Tomé, the English captain Robert Holmes noted both the high European mortality rate and its impact on the institution of marriage: "That which I took most notice of on this unfortunate shore was that all the women were in arms, formed into companies with captains, lieutenants and ensigns in good order, and 7 or 8 companies of them. The reason is that the males do not live long upon this island, but the females do, and they have 10 females for one male." Quoted in Richard Ollard, *Man of War: Sir Robert Holmes and the Restoration Navy* (London: Hodder and Stoughton, 1969), 122. Children of these unions between slave women and Portuguese men formed the powerful *parda* class (creole elite) that dominated local politics. Displaced from their native cultures, the African slave women not only were assimilated into Portuguese culture but also became the bearers of it to successive generations of mestizos. As an early observer remarked, "it sometimes happens that, when the [European] wife of a merchant dies, he takes a Negress, and this is an accepted practice, as the Negro population is both intelligent and rich, bringing up their daughters in our way of life, both as regards custom and dress. Children born of these unions are of a dark complexion and are called Mulattoes. They are

mischievous and difficult to manage." Charles R. Boxer, *Race Relations in the Portuguese Empire, 1415–1815* (Oxford: Clarendon Press, 1963), 15.

12. Jacobus Anne van der Chijs, *Nederlandsch-Indisch Plakaatboek, 1602–1811* [Dutch East Indies Book of Edicts, 1602–1811], 17 vols. (Batavia, 1888), 2:524 (hereafter cited as *PB* with volume number).

13. Bruijn, Gaastra, and Schöffer, *Dutch-Asiatic Shipping.*

14. Jan de Vries, "Connecting Europe and Asia: A Quantitative Analysis of the Cape Route Trade, 1497–1795" (unpublished paper).

15. Braudel, *Structures of Everyday Life,* 27.

16. Perhaps a more valid justification for European expansion might have been the benefits of empire to European cuisine. Left to its own endowment, Europe not only was without fine spices but also lacked a host of New World food products, central to dishes we now associate with Europe's "indigenous cuisine." Before conquistadors brought them to Europe, for example, Italians were without their tomato, Irish without their potato, and Belgians without their chocolate.

17. Archeological remains of Maluku cloves in Syria have been dated as early as 1700 B.C. The ancient trade with China was even more vigorous. Third-century Chinese accounts mention the Han emperor demanding that his courtiers have cloves in their mouth for fresher breath. Leonard Y. Andaya, *The World of Maluku: Eastern Indonesia in the Early Modern Period* (Honolulu: University of Hawaii Press, 1993).

18. See Leonard Y. Andaya, "The Lure of Spices," in Anthony Reid, ed., *Indonesian Heritage: Early Modern History* (Singapore: Editions Didier Millet-Archipelago Press, 1996); Barbara Watson Andaya and Leonard Andaya, *A History of Malaysia* (London: Macmillan, 1982).

19. In his famous 1934 book review, Jacob Cornelius van Leur wrongly emphasized the "peddling" or primitive nature of early modern Asian commerce in order to show that the commerce-centered European trading companies had little impact on the lives of ordinary Asians; see van Leur, *Indonesian Trade and Society.* Anthony Reid, *Expansion and Crisis,* volume 2 of *Southeast Asia in the Age of Commerce, 1450–1680* (New Haven: Yale University Press, 1993). For a response to van Leur see Marie Antoinette P. Meilink-Roelofsz, *Asian Trade and European Influence in the Indonesian Archipelago between 1500 and about 1630* (The Hague: Martinus Nijhoff, 1962).

20. For the details in my discussion of geography, I draw upon Reid, *Lands below the Winds.*

21. *Monsoon* is from the Arabic *mausim,* meaning "season."

22. Oliver Wolters, *Early Indonesian Commerce: A Study of the Origins of Srivijaya* (Ithaca, N.Y.: Cornell University Press, 1967), and *The Fall of Srivijaya in Malay History* (Ithaca, N.Y., Cornell University Press, 1970).

23. Sarnia Hayes Hoyt, *Old Malacca* (Kuala Lumpur: Oxford University Press, 1996), 9.

24. Andaya and Andaya, *History of Malaysia.*

25. Els M. Jacobs, *Koopman in Azië: De handel van de Verenigde Oost-Indische Compagnie tijdens de 18de eeuw* (Zutphen: Walburg Press, 2000), 27.

26. The Portuguese were on the cutting edge of fifteenth-century European naval technology. It was while on a Portuguese ship with his Portuguese wife off the Portuguese-held Canary Islands that Columbus noticed the westerly Canaries Current, which he hoped would lead him to Asia.

27. Niels Steensgaard, *The Asian Trade Revolution of the Seventeenth Century: The East India Companies and the Decline of the Caravan Trade* (Chicago: University of Chicago Press, 1974), 9. See also Frederic C. Lane, "The Mediterranean Spice Trade," *American Historical Review* 45 (1939–1940): 581.

28. The negative effects of squeezing the merchant classes too tightly would come back to haunt the Southeast Asian trading states as their dizzying heights at the beginning of the seventeenth century were matched only by their precipitous decline by century's end. This argument of the rise and fall of the Southeast Asian trading states is from Reid, *Expansion and Crisis*.

29. Steensgaard, *Asian Trade Revolution*, 92.

30. Femme S. Gaastra, in *De Geschiedenis van de VOC* (Leiden: Walburg Press, 1991), completely dispels the myth that it was Ottoman and Portuguese Spanish embargoes that drove the Dutch to Asia. It was, rather, simple undersupply.

31. Danish sound toll registers, logging each passing ship, are an important quantitative yardstick as well as the qualitative rants of Dutch competitors.

32. Jan de Vries and Ad van der Woude, *The First Modern Economy: Success, Failure, and Perseverance of the Dutch Economy, 1500–1815* (New York: Cambridge University Press, 1997), ch. 5.

33. Ibid. Most of the discussion of the Dutch economy here is based on the work of de Vries and van der Woude. The German sociologist Ferdinand Tonnies characterized gemeinschaft as (1) geographical isolation, (2) similarity among members, (3) the preeminence of tradition, (4) emphasis on consanguine family ties, (5) minimal division of labor, (6) an emphasis on ascribed status, (7) primary relationships, (8) a sense of the sacred. Gesellschaft, on the other hand, is characterized by (1) geographical mobility, (2) heterogeneity, (3) the decline of tradition, (4) emphasis on conjugal family ties, (5) division of labor resulting in hyper-individuality, (6) an emphasis on achieved status, (7) secondary relationships, (8) secularism.

34. Steensgaard, "The Companies," *Asian Trade Revolution*, ch. 3; de Vries and van der Woude, *First Modern Economy*, ch. 9.

35. Jacobs, *Koopman in Azië*, 11–12. This important new study details the expanse of the VOC and its worldwide trading presence.

36. Ibid., 18.

37. Leonard Andaya, *The Heritage of Arung Palakka: A History of South Sulawesi (Celebes) in the Seventeenth Century* (The Hague: Nijhoff, 1981).

38. Hasan Muarif Ambary, "Banten: From Pepper Port to Emporium," in *Early Modern History: Indonesian Heritage* (Singapore: Archipelago Press, 1999).

39. Bruijn, Gaastra, and Schöffer, *Dutch-Asiatic Shipping*; Jan de Vries, "Connecting Europe and Asia: A Quantitative Analysis of the Cape Route Trade, 1497–1795" (unpublished paper).

40. Jacobs, *Koopman in Azië*, 20.

41. Today the same phenomenon can be seen in modern nation states that have discovered it is more profitable to enrich a wider swath of their citizenry and tax their earnings than it is to monopolize wealth completely.

42. This severe fiscal practicality carried over into nineteenth-century colonial administration—well past the Company's demise—when slavery was abolished, less because it was morally wrong and more because it was costlier than coolie labor and the Cultivation System.

3 — COURTS AND COURTSHIP

1. R. W. Lee, *An Introduction to Roman-Dutch Law* (London: Oxford University Press, 1925).

2. A later Dutch jurist, Johannes van der Linden, commented on this process, "In order to answer the question what is the law in such and such a case we must first inquire whether any general law of the land or any local ordinance, having force of law, or any well-established custom, can be found affecting it. The Roman Law as a model of wisdom and equity is, in default of such a law, accepted by us through custom in order to supply this want." Johannes van der Linden, *Institutes of Holland*, translated by Henry Juta (Cape Town, 1884), 9.

3. A series of writings by Dutch jurists gave form to the fusion of Roman law with Dutch Germanic custom. Famous as the architect of international and maritime law, the Dutch jurist from Delft Hugo de Groot (Grotius) made the first and most influential summation of Roman Dutch law in *Inleiding tot de Hollandsche Rechtgeleertheyd*, published in English as Hugo Grotius, *The Jurisprudence of Holland*, ed. R. W. Lee (Oxford: Clarendon Press, 1936). Begun on 6 June 1619 (coincidentally, just six days after the Dutch governor general Jan P. Coen conquered Jakarta and found himself in need of a legal guide to govern), the *Jurisprudence* examined "the legal condition of persons" and property in a seventeenth-century context. Later Dutch jurists such as Simon van Leeuwen (1664), Johannes Voet (1698, 1704), D. G. van der Kessel (1800), and Johannes van der Linden (1806) published subsequent interpretations of Roman Dutch Law that continued to add nuance to the Dutch understanding of their civil code, a code that lasted until a French-inspired revolution brought an end to the old republic.

4. In 1809, the Napoleonic Code superseded Roman Dutch law in the new Batavian Republic (as the Netherlands was known in the wake of the French Revolution) and in its successor, the Kingdom of the Netherlands. A year later the

Netherlands were formally annexed by France. However, the Napoleonic Code was not a clean break from the Roman Dutch law. The Napoleonic Code was itself a compromise between the Germanic law and the Roman law, both of which had obtained in France before the Code. (Former Dutch colonies, most notably Sri Lanka and South Africa, still retain parts of Roman Dutch law in their legal system.)

5. *PB* 1:82.

6. Ibid., 99–100.

7. Ibid., 100.

8. Ibid., 89.

9. Ibid., 277. This seems to mirror the concern of later missionaries about the phenomenon of the so-called Rice Christian, that is, an Asian who converts to Christianity out of economic rather than spiritual motives.

10. *PB* 1:459.

11. Other "means to the advancement of the knowledge and the use of the Dutch language" were (1) to reward slaves with the privilege of wearing hats only "if they 'moderately understand and speak' the Dutch language, of which they must be able to show written verification, given by the Commissioners for Matrimonial Affairs. Otherwise their hat or cap will be confiscated and themselves be 'whipped soundly'"; (2) to "grant no letters of freedom [*vrij-brieven*]" to male or female slaves with Christian masters unless the slaves "had 'papers' [showing that they] could moderately speak the Dutch language." *PB* 1:460.

12. Ibid., 542.

13. All minors, said the Dutch jurists, must have a guardian. If a minor's parents were alive, the minor was under the guardianship of the parent. If, however, a minor's parents were deceased, the minor became a ward of the state. The state then either carried out the wishes of the parents regarding guardianship as stated in their will or, in the absence of such a testamentary provision, appointed a guardian. Statutes excluded some individuals from becoming guardians: women (excepting the ward's mother or grandmother), soldiers, and people who themselves had guardians. In the event that a suitable guardian (usually a family member) could not be found, the orphan (or *wees*) became a permanent ward of the state. At the orphanage (*weeshuis*) the *weesmeester* as the representative of the state became the orphan's legal guardian until the *weeskind* came of age. Directed to act in the interest of the minor, the guardian was to care for whatever estate the orphan may have received, represent the minor in court, teach the weeskind a trade, and see to his or her general well-being. Connected to the institution of the orphanhood was the *weeskamer* (Orphan Chamber), which functioned like the modern probate court. The weeskamer saw that a proper inventory was taken of the deceased's estate, made rulings on wills or intestate successions, and handled the devolution of the property in question. Especially in cities with large populations of weeskinderen, such as Amsterdam, the weeskamer became a powerful financial institution.

14. *PB* 1:513.

15. Grotius, *Jurisprudence*, 1.5.23.

16. Ibid.

17. This was proved a fiction in the Netherlands when, in the last quarter of the twentieth century, successive generations of Turks and Moroccans refused to return to their *buitenland* or to assimilate as Europeans. "Tolerance" was only a convenient civic religion when the virtual state of apartheid existed between Dutch and non Dutch in Netherlandic cities.

18. The Chinese alderman was called upon when a case involved a Chinese. It is unknown why, but Chinese served as aldermen in the eighteenth century (perhaps the VOC-sanctioned massacre of Batavian Chinese in 1741 was the watershed).

19. J. La Bree, *De Rechterlijke Organisatie en Rechtsbedeling te Batavia in de XVIIe Eeuw* (Rotterdam: Nijgh & Van Ditmar, 1951), 13. This title translates as "The legal structure and the administration of justice in Batavia in the seventeenth century."

20. John Ball, *Indonesian Legal History, 1602–1848* (Sydney: Oughtershaw Press, 1982), 9. Along with Ball's work, another overview of the Company legal structure is La Bree, *De Rechterlijke Organisatie*.

21. Reid, *Lands below the Winds*, 238.

22. This was a very different situation than in the South Pacific, for example, where traders could persuade local populations to hand over precious commodities for glass beads, iron nails, and other trinkets.

23. Leonard Andaya, "Cultural State Formation in Eastern Indonesia," in Anthony Reid, ed., *Southeast Asia in the Early Modern Era: Trade, Power, and Belief* (Ithaca, N.Y.: Cornell University Press, 1993).

24. Ball, *Indonesian Legal History*, 9.

25. *PB* 1:1–2.

26. Ibid., 6.

27. La Bree, *De Rechterlijke Organisatie*, 85.

28. *PB* 1:85; Jan Pietersz Coen, *Bescheiden omtrent zijn bedrijf in Indie*, ed. H. T. Colenbrander, 4 vols. (Den Haag, 1919–1922), 3:806.

29. Later, another prosecutor with the title "drossart der Bataviasche Ommelanden" (prosecutor of Batavia's environs) was added, to pursue non-Company crimes committed outside the walls of the city.

30. La Bree, *De Rechterlijke Organisatie*, 75. The tenets of the tangible ordered early Dutch Asia and race theory could only reign in social practice late in the 1800s, when it was wedded to capitalism. Like so many Europeans traveling to Asia, the mental baggage accompanying them seems also to have perished en route. This is not to say that Dutch Asia was a place that knew no prejudice; on the contrary, early modern Dutch Asia was rampant with collusion, discrimination, and intolerance. Batavia still had its bigotries, only they tended to be expressed in terms of Company status rather than race.

31. Urbanization in the Dutch Republic was at 40 percent, by far the highest in Europe, and 60 percent in Holland. Urbanization was fueled by the agricultural downturn in arable farming and a shift to livestock, creating an elastic supply of labor. See de Vries and van der Woude, *First Modern Economy*, chs. 6, 9, 13.

32. J. J. Orlers, *Beschrijvinge der Stadt Leyden* (Leiden, 1641), 619. Cited in the *Woordenboek der Nederlansche Taal* (Comprehensive Dutch Dictionary).

33. Coen, *Bescheiden omtrent zijn bedrijf in Indie*, 3:751, 980.

34. *PB* 1:92. For an example of this in action, see the case of Samuel Brandt (see Chapter 4) who allegedly kidnapped and kept the slavin Christina van Ambon. It was the gumshoe bailiff and his persistent kaffirs who tracked down Brandt and "liberated" Christina back into slavery.

35. In the seventeenth century, a Chinese alderman was called upon when a case involved a Chinese. Chinese did not serve as aldermen in the eighteenth century.

36. La Bree, *De Rechterlijke Organisatie*, 56.

37. Madie's life in Batavia had not been easy, but it had been improving steadily until his act of theft. From his name we assume he was from Mangarai on the island of Flores. In his examination, Madie said he had arrived in Batavia two years previously on a *Bugis prau* and since then had lived with a slave named Omar and worked as a coolie. Then he lived with a Portuguese named Queenis and worked as a servant boy, and finally, for the last six months he had lived with a woman named Magantie, who, Madie said, had taken him in as her own son and for whom he sold fish daily at the market. Examinatie van Madie vrij Mangarees voor Den Heer Landdrost Steven Poelman R: O: 14 March 1793, ff. 385–87, ARA 1.04.18.03, inv. 11981. On 15 April 1793, Madie was sentenced to be put in chains and to labor in ambachts quartier (so-called Artisans' District in Batavia) for five years.

38. My translation is from the contemporary Dutch translation in the records, Originele brief van den Tommongong Angadiridja van Bandong aan den heer Willem Vincent Helvicius van Riemsdijk, opperkoopman en gecommitteerden tot en over de zaaken van den Inlander, Aangebracht den 8 April 1778, ARA 1.04.18.03, inv. 11966.

39. Soeta confessed and was executed. We know he was hanged from a tiny drawing of a gallows next to his case. Eisch ad torturam door Trevijn contra Soeta, Javaan, 'S Heeren gevangen and anngeklaegde over manslag, 11 May 1778, ibid.

40. Damon was born in Batavia and was the freed slave of the former chair of the Justitie, Gijsbertus Maas, whom Damon accompanied on his repatriation to the Netherlands. When brought face-to-face with Damon in court, Tjoelan admitted not only that she knew him but that she had had a love affair with him before his departure to the Netherlands. After his return, Damon worked as a hireling for Tjoelan's mistress and lived in the house, but "however much Damon wanted to pick things up where they left off," wanting to be with her,

Tjoelan said, there was nothing going on between her and Damon or between her and a slave named Maas van Batavia. One day Damon discovered Tjoelan sitting on the stoop, talking and chewing betel with Maas. Damon quipped whether one wife was enough for Maas, a fight ensued, and Maas ended up mortally wounded.

41. The jurists debated the issue in a 142-point conclusion. Declaratoir nevens conclusie van Eijsch in cas crimineel van Casparus Hartman drossaart der Bataviasche Ommelanden Ratt: Off contra Damon van Batavia thans gedetineerde in den boeijen van desen gerecht als beschuldigt van manslag aan den slaaf Maas van Batavia geperpetreert, pages 114–49, ARA 1.04.18.03, inv. 11973.

42. Declaratoir van Adriana Philadelphia Thomas voor den heer landdrost Heeren Poelman R. Off: B: [pages 393–98], ARA 1.04.18.03, inv. 11976.

43. Regarding what "the Chinese fashion" of oath taking might be, this rare document describes the custom as cutting the head off of a stoen[?].

44. When Nio's father died, she did not have the means to bury him. The Chinese Lim Kienko (also spelled occasionally as Kinko) was coincidentally in the house of mourning, and out of charity and commiseration he offered to loan Nio the money to have her father buried, and Nio promised to pay him back. Lim repeatedly demanded to be paid back, and since Nio didn't have the money, she offered to go live with him. Lim agreed. He had a slavin named Balij van Balij with whom he had two children. In the beginning and for a while, apparently, Nio and Balij got along, but jealousy mounted, and daily quarrels and fights broke out, which eventually grew more violent. According to Nio, four days after the Chinese New Year while they were busy making preparations for a coming offering, Balij chased her children outside the house, locked the door from the inside, and took out the key. Balij came directly to the back, furiously gripping a hatchet she had retrieved from under the hearth of the cook shed, and delivered Nio four serious wounds. Nio said she went out of her mind with confusion and consternation, wanting to defend herself, threw a knife at the slavin injuring her in the crown of the head and lightly injuring the brain. Before she died, Balij said that Nio struck first.

45. Peranakan refers to someone of mixed Chinese and Malay/Indonesian heritage.

46. Batavia's famed insalubrity did not prevent some women from living well past the normal life expectancy in Dutch Asia. Octogenarians were not uncommon, and some even managed to approach the century mark. Nyai Saima was a "free, non-Christian," eighty-year-old Bimanese woman living just outside Batavia's Utrecht gate in an area called Godong Panjang. In general, court officials (to their credit) seemed more concerned with assessing the reliability of a witness, regardless of age, than automatically disqualifying a witness because of age (which was often only an approximation anyway).

47. Two took "an Islamic oath" and three took "a Chinese oath."

48. In a prosecutorial memo [*crimineel notul*] a request was made for *gijzeling* by the examination.

49. Declaratoir van de Chineese vrouw Lim Siongnio, D [pages 197–200], ARA 1.04.18.03, inv. 11976.

50. Tjoelan said that, shortly after her return from the Widow Lugthard's, she heard a loud scream in front of the door, and at the same time Tjoelan's mistress called out from across the way telling her to close the door. Tjoelan said she locked the door and from the window saw a great crowd of people gathered on the street. Damon lay on the ground and Maas was lying on top of Damon's body.

51. Maas coincidentally belonged to the senior merchant and bookkeeper general, Steven Poelman, who would later become the Drossaart (prosecutor) for the Schepenbank. Poelman told of the conversation he had had with Damon, who expressed despair ("What misfortune has come over me?") after the incident.

52. Tjoelan adds an interesting detail here, mentioning that Damon and Maas sat in front of Vos's house "on the step of Juff van der Poest who was living there." Apparently Juff van der Poest was the widow.

53. Later advocates against the onerous Cultivation System in the Netherlands Indies would also include speculative investors who saw the financial potential in ending formal slavery and instituting a new wage slavery.

4—BATAVIA AND ITS RUNAWAY SLAVINNEN

1. *Nyai* is a loosely and variously defined appellation for a common-law wife of an Asian man, or a housekeeper or live-in lover of European men; the title had many meanings, which also changed over time.

2. Djemal, Augusto, and another slave had agreed to share their wages from chopping wood, and it was Djemal's "bloody axe" that had led to Augusto's arrest. In a contemporary description of the Batavian plantation system, Ary Huysers describes the place of the *mandor*: "In this colony one must make do with slaves and bondsmen, under the supervision [of a] Mandoor, that will say foreman or supervisor over the slaves and plantation, the same as occurs in the West Indies." Ary Huysers, *Beknopte Beschrijving der Oostindische Etablissementen* (Amsteldam: Roos, 1792), 6.

3. [Attest Dauod Aboe Bakar 4 April 1793], pages 713–16, ARA 1.04.18.03, inv. 11982.

4. Anthony Reid, "Introduction" in *Slavery, Bondage, and Dependency in Southeast Asia,* ed. Anthony Reid (New York: St. Martin's Press, 1983), 14.

5. See Reid, *Slavery, Bondage, and Dependency.*

6. A modern example might be the professoriate in Europe. Rather than working full-time for one research university, many academics have, for example, a partial appointment at one university, a partial appointment at another, a post at a research institute, and a consulting business on the side with its own clients.

7. Reid, "Introduction" to *Slavery, Bondage, and Dependency*, 8.

8. For specific examples in a variety of Southeast Asian contexts, see Reid, *Southeast Asia in the Early Modern Era.*

9. Benedict R. O'G. Anderson, "The Idea of Power in Javanese Culture," in *Culture and Politics in Indonesia*, ed. Claire Holt (Ithaca, N.Y.: Cornell University Press, 1972), 28.

10. For a sustained treatment on the interplay of power and patronage in Southeast Asia, see Scott, *Moral Economy of the Peasant*, Scott, *Domination and the Arts of Resistance,* and James C. Scott, *Weapons of the Weak: Everyday Forms of Peasant Resistance* (New Haven: Yale University Press, 1985).

11. Aung Thwin cited in Reid, *Slavery, Bondage, and Dependency*, 8.

12. Anderson, "Power in Javanese Culture," 34.

13. See the chapter "Some Features of the Cultural Matrix" in Oliver W. Wolters, *History, Culture, and Region in Southeast Asian Perspectives* (Ithaca: SEAP, 1999), 15–40.

14. Reid, "Introduction," in *Slavery, Bondage, and Dependency*, 13.

15. The term "civil law" can be confusing because it can be used correctly in two separate instances. One usage (the one used here) applies to the distinction between civil law versus common law, the two broad categorizations of legal practice. Civil law (which relies on a comprehensive law code rather than legal precedent) is, for example, the legal tradition used by much of continental Europe; common law (typified by juries and reliance on case law) is the foundation of all legal practice in the United States and Great Britain, for example. In its second usage, civil law is also used to distinguish between "civil" matters (such as contracts, property, marriage, and so on) and criminal matters, a distinction that appears in both common law and civil law traditions.

16. Paul Mus, *India Seen from the East: Indian and Indigenous Cults in Champa* (Clayton, Victoria: Monash University, Centre of Southeast Asian Studies, 1975); Wolters, *History, Culture, and Region.*

17. Reid, "Introduction," *Slavery, Bondage, and Dependency*, 13.

18. In Gouw Tjansie's declarant, Jiemoen [also Joeman, Jiemon] is referred to as an inlander and in Jiemoen's own declarant we find that he swears by his testimony "in Islamic fashion." He lived with his mother near the lime kilns. A rijksdaalder was a coin worth two and a half guilders. Declaratoir van Gouw Tjansie luijtenand der Chineese natie voor den heer Landdrost Steven Poelman Ratt: Off: B: [pages 252–59], ARA 1.04.18.03, inv. 11977.

19. Eijsch ad Mortem nevens mindere eijschen conclusie crimineel item declaratoir den heer Landdrost Steven Poelman Ratt: Off: Eijschr contra Amien C:S: 'S Heeren gev: [pages 188–89], ARA 1.04.18.03, inv. 11977.

20. At the request of Gouw Tjansie, mata mata later shadowed one of the jewelry fences to a Chinese goldsmith who was melting down the precious metal. [Decl Tjinde 22 September 1791], ARA 1.04.18.03, inv. 11977.

21. A schelling was a silver coin worth six stivers.

22. Inform Akier 11 October 1791, ARA 1.04.18.03, inv. 11977.

23. Eijsch 15 December 1791; Decl Danie 22 September 1791, ibid.

24. He was charged as an accessory to the kidnapping and sentenced to a severe lashing, to be branded, chained, and sent to labor in the Ambachts quarter for fifty years.

25. This revelation came only after Amien had given up on an earlier story where he claimed that Lepo had approached him to help bring a sick sister to the *dukun* (medicine man) with Akier's boat; after Amien and Lepo picked up the girl, Lepo disembarked with his "sister" but returned alone.

26. The distiller was named Lim Konghiem. In 1778, writer Ary Huysers counted twenty rice-wine distilleries (*Araksbranderyen*) in Batavia. Huysers, *Oostindische Etablissementen.*

27. Both Mingo and Laijseeng were freed slaves, Mingo from a Nyai Mina and Laijseeng from a Tan Hoelo. Mata mata sent out by the highest-ranking captain of the Chinese nation, Ong Tjoeseeng, shadowed Laijseeng to the Chinese goldsmith and retrieved the pieces from him there.

28. Eijsch 15 December 1791, ARA 1.04.18.03, inv. 11982.

29. [Decl Sara 9 July 1777], ARA 1.04.18.03, inv. 11965. Walburg was a VOC merchant and died while Christina was a fugitive. Coincidentally, the Schepenbank also oversaw estate sales, and the estate belonged to a Jan Marchant Carelsz, who had purchased Christina from someone whose name was abbreviated as "d'E S'Glain."

30. [Decl Christina van Ambon 1 July 1777], ibid.

31. Knowing that Brandt was involved but without proof of Christina's whereabouts, Sara and her husband filed so many formal complaints that an "exasperated" bailiff finally ordered his kaffirs to bring Brandt to Sara's house for questioning. Interrogators, including regular civilians, fired questions at Brandt. In one heated exchange, Brandt's former neighbor from the Rua Novo said, "Give up the girl. Where is she? Put an end to the matter," to which Brandt exploded, "Did I kidnap the girl!? Can you prove that I took her out of the house?" [Decl Sara 9 July 1777], ARA 1.04.18.03, inv. 11965.

32. [Decl Hodenpijl-Klok-Bouwman 17 July 1777], ibid.

33. The tip came from Jurgen Fredrik van der Klok who had been avidly following the case. Van der Klok was a burgher who "coincidentally" happened to be perched in a tree in his father-in-law's yard picking star fruit (*belimbing*) when he saw a woman in Brandt's house dressed in a short blouse (Malay, *cabaij, kebaya*) whom he had never before seen at the door. He sought out others (apart from Sara or the authorities) who had an interest in the case, even finding someone who had known Christina to see if his description matched. When Sara's nephew Ruijsch asked for van der Klok's help, he took them to his father-in-law's and let them spy on Brandt, also mentioning that he had seen the girl several times while trying to

spy through Brandt's wall panels. From their perch, Ruijsch spotted the girl on 20 December, and the kaffirs moved in on the house two days later. Sara's nephew was Fredrik Hendrik Ruijsch, a VOC bookkeeper for the military.

34. [Decl Dulla 1 July 1777], ARA 1.04.18.03, inv. 11965. Dulla was a shortened form of Abdullah; "sissy" in Dutch was *susje* or *zusje.*

35. In the court papers, there is a "provision for flogging" (*provisie van gijseling*) made before the sentence itself. Normally appearing in sentencing, the phrase *strengelijk gegeesselt* succinctly defines both the method and the mode of the flogging. *Strengelijk* is rendered as "severe" in English; *Gegeesselt* has as its root the noun *geesel*, which is an Old Dutch word defined by the *Woordenboek der Nederlandsche Taal* as "an instrument of punishment for disciplining offenders or for self-castigation, consisting of small ropes whose ends are equipped with knobs, lead loads or iron thorns, for lashing the back and the haunches bloody." The *geesel* is the infamous whip known in English as the cat-o'-nine-tails.

36. [Exam Brandt 12 July 1777], ARA 1.04.18.03, inv. 11965.

37. [Notul 18 July 1777], ibid.

38. [Consideratien 29 October 1777], ibid.

39. The criminal sentence is missing from the archival bundle so we do not know their punishment.

40. [Crim. Eijsch 26 February 1787], ARA 1.04.18.03, inv. 11972.

41. [Decl. Poedak 5 January 1787], [Crim. Eijsch 26 February 1787], ibid.

42. Ambary, "Banten."

43. Raben, "Batavia and Colombo."

44. *PB* 2:227–28.

45. Buitenzorg shared the same name, founding date, and ideals as Prussia's Sans Soucis, the summer palace built by the "enlightened despot" Fredrick II in Potsdam. But instead of building a German "Chinese Tea House" as Fredrick the Great did to remind him of a fantastic Orient, Java's "Without Cares" palace was surrounded by the actual "East," and Buitenzorg was meant as a reminder of an "Occident," a place just as fantastic for the European born or living in the Indies as the East was for Fredrick and company. Buitenzorg is modern-day Bogor.

46. [Decl. Poedak 5 January 1787], [Decl. Saringtang 5 January 1787], ARA 1.04.18.03, inv. 11972.

47. [Crim. Eijsch 26 February 1787], ARA 1.04.18.03, inv. 11972. *Bapak* is a polite term of address or generic title for man, often older. In the records, *Bapak* was often spelled phonetically as *Bappa.*

48. In this particular criminal case, the knife is described as a *clewang* and also as *parring* (in Malay, *parang*, meaning "cleaver"). Elsewhere *gollok, klewang,* and *parang* are used interchangeably.

49. [Crim. Eijsch 26 February 1787], ARA 1.04.18.03, inv. 11972.

50. The *Woordenboek der Nederlansche Taal* defines *laarzen* as the "name for a form of punishment used previously aboard ship whereby a sailor, consequent

to a legal judgment, was castigated with a length of rope on the backside."

51. [Crim. Eijsch 26 February 1787], ARA 1.04.18.03, inv. 11972. It is implied that Poedak, though in chains for a year, would be earning an independent wage from which to pay that fine.

52. In the records, *Sheik* often appeared phonetically as *Sjech*.

53. Examinatie van Sitie van Maccassar 'S Heeren gev: voor den heer Landdrost Steven Poelman Ratt: Off:/ F, 5 October 1792, ARA 1.04.18.03, inv. 11979. Unless otherwise noted, quotes and statements from the subsequent account are from Sitie's interrogation.

54. Sitie said it transpired "some months" before her interrogation on 5 October 1792; Sheik Nannekoe puts the date of the toothache at a little over two months before October 5.

55. Crimineele Notul de dato 1 October 1792 voor de Wel Ed. Agtb Heer Landdrost Steeven Poelman R:O:/ A, ARA 1.04.18.03, inv. 11979. Clerks transcribed *Kyai* phonetically as *Kiaij* or *Keaij*.

56. James R. Fox, ed., *Indonesian Heritage: Religion and Ritual* (Singapore: Editions Didier Millet–Archipelago Press, 1999).

57. Exam Sitie 5 October 1792, ARA 1.04.18.03, inv. 11979.

58. Crimineele Eijsch en conclusie door heer Steven Poelman drossaart der Bataviasche Ommelanden RO Eijsch contra Abas—Javaan CS. 'S Heeren gev: [28 March 1791, pages 573–84], ARA 1.04.18.03, inv. 11979.

59. Declaratoir van Sjech Nannekoe moor voor den heer Landdrost Steven Poelman Ratt: Off:/ B [5 October 1792], ibid.

60. *Ma Aijo* (also spelled *Aaijo*) lived by the bridge on the Ankeeseweg. Her legal name, the record states, was Rahaio.

61. Verbaal van Enquesten den heer Steven Poelman drossaart den Bataviasche ommelanden Ratt Off contra Sitie van macasser, heeren comm Engelhard, Martheze adjt Lorh, Smit [23 October 1792], ARA 1.04.18.03, inv. 11979.

62. We know this about Nyai Janna, because in her statement she signed with a mark, and she swore an oath in the "Mohammedanic fashion," which from other court documents was described as putting one's right hand on the Koran.

63. The Company not only arrived in Asia seeking to situate itself into a preexisting, fully functional, international commercial network but also stepped into an established world of diplomatic protocols, conspicuous consumption, and cultural performance, within which it sought fluency and legitimization. Alongside the formalized Asian and Southeast Asian exchange of diplomatic letters and detailed court protocols in which the VOC engaged, on a broader individual level, Company men and non-Company merchants worked tirelessly to assemble and display the plumage and playthings of the leisure class. In Asia, there existed none of the sober "embarrassment of riches" believed to have hung like the perpetual cloud over the early modern Netherlands. See Simon Schama, *The Embarrassment of Riches: An Interpretation of Dutch Culture in the Golden Age*

(Berkeley and Los Angeles: University of California Press, 1988).

64. We do not know whether the phrase "acting like" is an editorial insertion by the sworn court clerk, Johanes Lohr, or whether Sitie did not in fact think she was a "woman of privilege."

65. The scribe Oeij Loanko may have needed to supplement his income by pawn brokering, because he signed his deposition with a very sloppy mark, imitating a Chinese character. The same holds for the scribe Na Kienseeng.

66. The official Dutch title is drossaert der Bataviasche Ommelanden, Ratt. Off. (ratione officii).

67. Siberg, like most presidents of the Court of Aldermen, was also a full member of the Indies Council, the highest authority in the Dutch East Indies.

68. In the Roman Dutch law, the first charge of endangerment (*bedreigeschijen*) can apply not only to endangering lives but also to endangering property. In legal parlance the second vague charges of other offenses (*wanbedorijt, wanbedrijf*) usually meant that the alleged crime did not warrant capital punishment or life imprisonment but was a lesser crime.

69. Some of the items were a gold rupee; Nyai Janna's clothes, buttons, and medallion; three of Ma Aijo's sarongs; Tsikini's buttons; and fifty rijksdaalders from goods pawned to Bapak Salee. A different Salee, this one a dukun, was to have received a sarong as payment for medicine. Sitie sent another sarong to her sister in Makasar, perhaps hoping to follow it home. Had this been a "pure" escape attempt like others chronicled here, we would have seen more of her ill-gotten gain going toward her flight and her new life. Sitie was instead being used by the dukun to further his own interests.

70. Ranati professed her husband's innocence, though the aldermen thought Ranati "not in a state to do it [that is, testify] chiefly because of her advanced age, which was judged to be at least 80, despite willingness to place her denial next to that of her husband. Despite her advanced age she is very suspect based on that which was said about her by Sitie . . . [yet because of her advanced age] the officers of the court will not pursue any [legal] action against this woman." Verbaal [23 October 1792], ARA 1.04.18.03, inv. 11979.

71. For her second visit, Kyai Dukun said that Sitie arrived in the coach of the city auctioneer Heemskerk. Her explanation was that one night while she was living with Kyai Dukun, Sitie was returning from the market when an unspecified attempt was made on her life. Sitie continued traveling most of the night by boat, finally stopping by Heemskerk's plantation where she disembarked and hid for the night. Sitie told Heemskerk that Kyai Dukun "was a healer," and in the morning the auctioneer's coachman brought her back to the dukun. The medicine man went in person to thank the coachman for his trouble.

72. Exam Sitie 5 October 1792, ARA 1.04.18.03, inv. 11979. Supposing Sitie's story to be true and that Kyai Dukun was not simply her fall guy, she was in the terrible position of being conscious of what was happening to her but unable to control it.

73. Examinatie van Sitjoe de Wangsa 'S Heeren gev: voor den heer Landdrost Steven Poelman Ratt Off [23 October 1792], ARA 1.04.18.03, inv. 11979. Kyai Dukun denied ever wearing the documents and instead rather randomly insisted that a pair of gold buttons recently found in the Stadhuis garbage pile were his and were on his shirt when he was brought into jail. Regarding Sitjoe's magical abilities, drossart Steven Poelman noted his "sorcery" and his "incomprehensible power" over Sitie. "Kyai Dukun through many, very many peculiar happenings appears to know something of the black and dangerous magic of which Sitie admits to have become a victim." But in "supernatural affairs," he defers "to wise understandings [that is, the Schepenen] and the much more enlightened judgment" without making his "feelings public concerning matters so unusual and dark."

74. This did not mean, however, that the Schepenbank would overlook her financial misconduct. Poelman wrote that "all acts of this nature must be considered so that they do not go unpunished [because] a slave is treated more severely than a free person as in this instance when they [perpetrate the crimes] at the expense of a legal master and commit a kind of domestic theft."

75. [Crim Eijsch 10 December 1792], ARA 1.04.18.03, inv. 11979.

76. Ibid.

77. Reid, "Introduction," *Slavery, Bondage, and Dependency*, 8.

78. "Confessie van Panjang, Javaan" [7 June 1792], ARA 1.04.18.03, inv. 11979.

79. Crimineele Eijsch en Conclusie den heer Steven Poelman drossaert den Bataviasche ommelanden Ratt Off Eijschen contra Panjang—Javaen C:S: 'S Heeren gev: over domestique diefte met braak verseld [17 December 1792], ibid.

80. Crimineele Eijsch en Conclusie [17 December 1792], ARA 1.04.18.03, inv. 11979.

81. Confessie van Serijam, Javaan [7 June 1792], ibid.

82. Confessie van Esperanca van Boegis, [7 June 1792], ibid. The remainder of Esperanca's quotations are also from this document.

83. They may have lived in a typical two-story Dutch colonial home for there was rarely any discussion of upstairs or downstairs in Asian houses. (And for those who slept upstairs, it may have saved their lives. There is evidence that some of the mosquito-borne diseases of Batavia never struck those sleeping in a second-floor bedroom out of the range of the female *anophales* mosquito.) If Esperanca is telling the truth, they took an incredible risk, stealing a chest and other items from her mistress while upstairs on the same floor. Kuvel's wife reported that Esperanca indeed came to her upstairs asking for money to buy bread and butter.

84. Verbaal van Enquesten door Steven Poelman drossaert der Bataviasche Ommelanden Ratt Off contra Esperance van boegis C:S:, ARA 1.04.18.03, inv. 11979.

85. Abdul and Slamien said that they were not *waronghouders* but described how they made their meager livelihood by renting out a space in front of their

front door to a "small warong of little importance." Verbaal van Enquesten, ARA 1.04.18.03, inv. 11979.

86. Crimineele Eijsch en Conclusie [17 December 1792], ibid.

87. While Isabelle lay dying and Esperanca and the stablemen were detained in jail, Sitie had fled from Nannekoe and was anxiously racking up enormous consumer debt. The sentences against Sitie and Esperanca were carried out on the same day.

88. Surprisingly, Esperanca was given only half the sentence that her accomplices received.

89. Reid, "Introduction," *Slavery, Bondage, and Dependency*, 16, 14.

5—GENDER, ABUSE, AND THE MODERN WORLD SYSTEM

1. Karl Marx and Frederick Engels, *The Communist Manifesto*, ed. Eric Hobsbawm (New York: Verso, 1998), 38.

2. Declaratoir van de slavinn Tjindra van Balij voor den Heer Jan Hendrik Poock Ratt. Off No. 2 [1 May 1775], ARA 1.04.18.03, inv. 11963.

3. Nieuwe schelling [Decl. Tjindra 1 May 1775], ibid. A daily wage would have been one-twentieth of a pound.

4. [Decl. Tjindra 1 May 1775], ibid.

5. Crimiineelen Eijsh door Jan Hendrik Poock, Drostaert den Bataviase ommelanden Rat^e ofte Eijsschen contra Oetan parnakan Chineese vrouw wijff van der vrij Balien Amat gedaegdesse. Op 't mishandele van haar slavinne Tjindra van Balij, 26 June 1775, ibid.

6. [Decl. Oetan, 22 May 1775] and Notul de dato 26 Junij 1775 voor Jan Hendrik Poock rat off eijsch contra Oetan parnakan Chieneese vrouw gedaagdesse, ibid.

7. [Decl. Tjindra 1 May 1775] and [Verkl. Beijlon 25 April 1775], ibid. In the last half of the eighteenth century, city surgeons made the decent wage of eighty rijksdaalders per month. See Huysers, *Oostindische Etablissementen*.

8. [Decl. Oetan, 22 May 1775], ARA 1.04.18.03, inv. 11963.

9. [Compareerde Oetan, 26 May 1775], ibid.

10. [Crim. Eijsh 26 June 1775], ibid.

11. Appointement voor den agtb heer Jan Hendrik Poock drosaart der Bataviasch ommelande Ratt Off Eijs contra Oelan geda.se, no. 1, 10 July 1775, ibid.

12. [Crim. Eijsh 26 June 1775], ibid.

13. Declaratoir Mono van Boegis, 31 July 1765, ibid.

14. [Decl. Boegis 31 July 1765], ibid.

15. Declaratoir van Tan Kiok van Manilla C:S: [that is, Tan Biouko] voor den heer Bailluw David Julius van Aitsma Rat: Off: 9 October 1777, ibid., inv. 11966.

16. Ende on the island of Flores.

17. [Decl. Kiok-Biouko 9 October 1777], ARA 1.04.18.03, inv. 11966.

18. No title [Exam. Ontong 30 August 1777], ibid.

19. No title [Crim. Eijsch Balliuw David Julius van Aitsma, 29 September 1777], ibid.

20. No title [Decl. Sabil-Bintje, 3 March 1778], ibid.

21. Examinatie van Tapesan van Balij, 3 March 1778, ibid.

22. [Exam. Tapesan 3 March 1778], ibid.

23. Ibid.

24. [Decl. Sabil-Bintje, 3 March 1778], ibid.

25. Notul 2 March 1778 for Jan Hendrik Trevijn drossart der Bataviase ommelanden Rat: Off:, ibid.

26. No title [Sur. Attest Beijlon 2 March 1778], ibid.

27. By hanging. [Notul Trevijn 2 March 1778], ibid.

28. *Mond trommel*, some sort of percussion instrument played on the mouth.

29. Examinatie van Laka van Timor, 'S Heeren gev voor de heer Jan Hendrik Poock drossaert der Bataviasche ommelanden ratt off, no. 3, 18 March 1777, ARA 1.04.18.03, inv. 11965.

30. Kiauwa's version is backed up by Tan Koko who saw Laka walking around "half-naked." Another of Tan Koko's slaves, Laijkoeij van Siam, and his free Balinese friend Adjie gave similar testimony. Tan Koko signed his deposition in Roman script, Laijkoeij signed with an "X," and perhaps Adjie was a haji for he signed in Arabic script. Declaratoir van Tan Kocko C:S: [that is, Laijkoeij van Siam and Adjie] voor de heer Jan Hendrik Poock Rat: Off: no. 2, 18 March 1777, ibid.

31. Declaratoir van Kiauwa van Passier voor den heer landdrost Jan Hendrik Poock, no. 5, 8 April 1777, ibid.

32. [Exam. Laka 18 March 1777], ibid.

33. Crimineelen Eijsch door Jan Hendrik Poock drossaert der Bataviasche ommelanden Rat Off Eijscher contra Laka van Timor slaaf van den Chin. Tan Kocko SHG over voorgenomen selfs moord en questing, ibid.

34. Crimineele Versoek door Steven Poelman drossaart der Bataviasche ommelanden Ratt: Off: contra Sinliang van Balij 'S Heeren gev: 8 April 1793, ARA 1.04.18.03, inv. 11981.

35. [Crim. Versoek 8 April 1793], ibid.

36. Examinatie van Sinliang van Balij voor Den Heer Landdrost Steven Poelman R: O:, 20 December 1792, ibid.

37. Declaratoir van Mauwar van Sumbauwa vrije gegeevene slavinne en Sioralia van Balij voor Den Heer Landdrost Steven Poelman R: O:, 20 December 1792, ibid, ff. 277–78.

38. [Exam. Sinliang 20 December 1792], ibid.

39. Ibid.

40. Het Chirurginaal Attest, ibid., ff. 273; Declaratoir van Oeij Tjungkong Chin voor Den Heer Landdrost Steven Poelman R: O:, ibid, ff. 275–76; [Decl. van Mauwar-Sioralia 20 December 1792], ibid., ff. 277–78.

41. [Decl. Oeij], ibid., f. 276.

42. [Crim. Versoek Sinliang 8 April 1793], ibid.

43. Sentencie Crimineel voor Den Heer Landdrost Steven Poelman R: O: contra Siliang van Balij 'S Heeren gev: [15 April 1793], ibid.

44. Declaratoir van Hang Kienio wede van Ong Tjoeseeng [18 September 1793], ARA 1.04.18.03, inv. 11983, ff. 49–52.

45. Before the court, Letjong was treated as a free person. He also swore an Islamic oath before the court.

46. Huysers, *Oostindische Etablissementen*, 146–72.

47. Informatie van Tjambang van Maccasser 'S Heeren geve over quetsing van zijn lijfvrouw C:S: voor den Achtb Heer Landt: Steven Poelman Ratt Off, [2 November 1793], ARA 1.04.18.03, inv. 11983, ff. 81–90.

48. Declaratoir van Intje Soekoe C.S. [21 September 1793], ibid., ff. 65–70. Luckily the wound just pierced the skin and was later judged "inconsequential" by the surgeon. Chirurgienal Attest den door den gev. Slaaf Tjembang aan verscheijden perzoonen toegebragt wonden [18 September 1793], ibid., ff. 47–48.

49. Declaratoir van de slavinne Teta van Boegis [18 September 1793], ibid., ff. 53–56.

50. [Decl Hang Kienio 18 September 1793], ibid., ff. 49–52.

51. Declaratoir van Gouw Tjansie [18 September 1793], ibid., ff. 61–64.

52. Examen van Tjambang van Maccasser S.H. gev [18 September 1793], ibid., ff. 57–60.

53. Eijsch en Conclusie ter scherper examen van Steven Poleman drossaart der Bataviasche ommelanden Ratt: Off: contra Tjambang van Macasser 'S Heeren gev: over moetwillige kwetzing bijweege van amock [3 Oct 1793], ibid., ff. 39–42.

54. Crimineele Eijsch en Conclusie van Steven Poleman Ratt: Off: contra Tjambang van Macasser C:S: S Heeren gev: [1 December 1793], ibid., ff. 5–30.

55. [2nd] Informatie van Tjambang van Maccasser 'S Heeren geve over quetsing van zijn lijfvrouw C:S: voor den Achtb Heer Landt: Steven Poelman Ratt Off, [2 November 1793], ibid., ff. 91–100.

56. Sentencie Crimineele voor den Heer Landdrost Steven Poleman Eijsch: Ratt: Off: contra Tjambang van Macasser C:S: S Heeren geve: [no date], ibid., ff. 1–4.

CONCLUSION

1. R. E. Elson, *The End of the Peasantry in Southeast Asia: A Social and Economic History of Peasant Livelihood, 1800–1990s* (New York: St. Martin's, 1997), 36.

2. The Dutch had created the idea of a Dutch East Indies, a single archipelago-wide entity, and natives across the island chain began to unite for the first time as Indonesians, galvanized by this new national identity and a common disenchantment with the Dutch colonial presence. Japanese occupation

of Southeast Asia in World War II expelled the Dutch and gave Indonesians the firm footing to resist Dutch attempts at re-conquest from 1945 to 1949, when the Dutch finally recognized Indonesia's independence.

3. John S. Furnivall, *Netherlands India: A Study of Plural Economy* (Cambridge: Cambridge University Press, 1939), xvi.

4. Mason C. Hoadley, *Selective Judicial Competence: The Cirebon-Priangan Legal Administration, 1680–1792* (Cornell: Southeast Asia Program Studies, 1994).

5. The Ethici are scholars and colonial officials who came of age in the wake of colonial change initiated by the publication of works such as Max Havelaar and other liberal-minded calls for reform.

6. Daniel S. Lev, "Judicial Institutions and Legal Culture in Indonesia," in *Culture and Politics in Indonesia*, ed. Claire Holt (Ithaca: Cornell University Press, 1972), 246–318 (254).

Bibliography

Abeyasekere, Susan. *Jakarta: A History.* Singapore: Oxford University Press, 1989.

Algra, N. E., and H. R. W. Gokkel. *Verwijzend en verklarend juridisch woordenboek.* 7de druk. Alphen aan den Rijn: Samsom H. D. Tjeenk Willink, 1994.

Ambary, Hasan Muarif. "Banten: From Pepper Port to Emporium." In Reid, *Early Modern History,* 50–51.

Andaya, Barbara Watson. "Cash Cropping and Upstream-Downstream Tensions: The Case of Jambi in the Seventeenth and Eighteenth Centuries." In Reid, *Southeast Asia in the Early Modern Era: Trade, Power, Belief,* 91–122.

———. "The Changing Religious Role of Women in Pre-modern South East Asia." *South East Asia Research* 2, no. 2 (September 1994): 99–116.

———. *The Flaming Womb: Repositioning Women in Early Modern Southeast Asia.* Honolulu: University of Hawaii Press, 2006.

———. "From Temporary Wife to Prostitute: Sexuality and Economic Change in Early Modern Southeast Asia." *Journal of Women's History* 9, no. 4 (1998): 11–34.

———, ed. *Other Pasts: Women, Gender, and History in Early Modern Southeast Asia.* Honolulu: Center for Southeast Asian Studies, University of Hawaii, Manoa, 2000.

———. "Women and Economic Change: The Pepper Trade in Pre-modern Southeast Asia." *Journal of the Economic and Social History of the Orient* 38, no. 2 (1995): 165–90.

Andaya, Barbara Watson, and Leonard Andaya. *A History of Malaysia.* London: Macmillan, 1982.

Andaya, Leonard Y. "The Bugis-Makassar Diasporas." *Journal of the Malaysian Branch of the Royal Asiatic Society* 68, no. 1 (1995): 119–38.

———. *The Heritage of Arung Palakka: A History of South Sulawesi (Celebes) in the Seventeenth Century.* The Hague: Nijhoff, 1981.

———. "The Lure of Spices." In Reid, *Indonesian Heritage: Early Modern History.*

———. "'A Very Good-Natured but Awe-Inspiring Government': The Reign of a Successful Queen in Seventeenth-Century Aceh." In *Hof en Handel: Aziatische Vorsten in de VOC 1620–1720,* 59–84. Leiden: KITLV Press, 2004.

———. *The World of Maluku: Eastern Indonesia in the Early Modern Period.* Honolulu: University of Hawaii Press, 1993.

Anderson, Benedict R. O'G. "The Idea of Power in Javanese Culture." In *Culture and Politics in Indonesia,* ed. Claire Holt, 1–70. Ithaca, N.Y.: Cornell University Press, 1972.

Apeldoorn, L. J. van. *Geschiedenis van het Nederlandsche Huwelijksrecht voor de Invoering van de Fransche Wetgeving.* Amsterdam: Holland, 1925.

Atkinson, Jane Monnig, and Shelly Errington, eds. *Power and Difference: Gender in Island Southeast Asia.* Stanford, Calif.: Stanford University Press, 1990.

Ball, John. *Indonesian Legal History, 1602–1848.* Sydney: Oughtershaw Press, 1982.

Bemmelen, Sita van, Madelon Djajadingrat-Niewenhuis, Elsbeth Locher-Scholten, and Elly Touwen-Bouwsma, eds. *Women and Mediation in Indonesia.* Leiden: KITLV Press, 1992.

Benda, Harry J. "The Structure of Southeast Asian History: Some Preliminary Observations." *Journal of Southeast Asian History* 3, no. 1 (March 1962): 106–39.

Berk, P. J. W. van der. *Latijn bij genealogisch onderzoek.* Den Haag: Centraal Bureau voor genealogie, 1997.

Blussé, Leonard. *Bitters Bruid: Een Koloniaal Huwelijksdrama in de Gouden Eeuw.* Amersfoort: Balans, 1997.

———. *Strange Company: Chinese Settlers, Mestizo Women, and the Dutch in VOC Batavia.* Dordrecht: Foris, 1986.

Blussé, Leonard, and Femme Gaastra, eds. *On the Eighteenth Century as a Category of Asian History: Van Leur in Retrospect.* Singapore: Ashgate, 1998.

Boey, Thymon. *Woorden-tolk: of verklaring der voornaamste onduitsche en andere woorden in de hedendaagsche een aaloude rechtspleginge voorkoomende mitsgaders korte schets.* 'S-Gravenhage: Johannes Gaillard, 1773.

Boomgaard, Peter. *Children of the Colonial State: Population Growth and Economic Development in Java, 1795–1880.* Amsterdam: Free University Press, 1989.

Boserup, Ester. *Women's Role in Economic Development.* New York: St. Martin's Press, 1970.

Boxer, Charles R. *The Dutch Seaborne Empire, 1600–1800.* New York: Knopf, 1965.

———. *Mary and Misogyny: Women in Iberian Expansion Overseas, 1415–1815; Some Facts, Fancies, and Personalities.* London: Duckworth, 1975.

———. *Race Relations in the Portuguese Empire, 1415–1815.* Oxford: Clarendon Press, 1963.

Braudel, Fernand. *Civilization and Capitalism, 15th–18th Century: The Structures of Everyday Life.* Berkeley and Los Angeles: University of California Press, 1992.

———. *The Structures of Everyday Life: The Limits of the Possible.* New York: Perennial Library, 1981.

Brug, P. H. van der. *Malaria en Malaise: De VOC in Batavia in de achttiende eeuw.* Amsterdam: De Bataafsche Leeuw, 1994.

Bruijn, J. R., F. S. Gaastra, and I. Schöffer. *Dutch-Asiatic Shipping in the Seventeenth and Eighteenth Centuries.* The Hague: Martinus Nijhoff, 1987.

Carey, Peter, and Vincent Houben. "Spirited Srikandhis and Sly Sumbadras: The

Social, Political and Economic Role of Women at the Central Javanese Courts in the Eighteenth and Early Nineteenth Centuries." In Locher-Scholten and Niehof, *Indonesian Women in Focus,* 12–42.

Chijs, Jacobus Anne van der. *Nederlandsch-Indisch Plakaatboek, 1602–1811.* 17 vols. Batavia: Landsdrukkerij, 1885–1900.

Clancy-Smith, Julia, and Frances Gouda, eds. *Domesticating the Empire: Race, Gender, and Family Life in French and Dutch Colonialism.* Charlottesville: University Press of Virginia, 1998.

Coen, Jan Pietersz. *Bescheiden omtrent zijn bedrijf in Indie.* Edited by H. T. Colenbrander. 4 vols. Den Haag: Nijhoff, 1919–1922.

Cooper, Frederick, and Ann Laura Stoler, eds. *Tensions of Empire: Colonial Cultures in a Bourgeois World.* Berkeley and Los Angeles: University of California Press, 1997.

Couperus, Louis. *The Hidden Force: A Story of Modern Java.* Translated by Alexander Teixeira de Mattos. New York: Dodd, 1921.

Crawfurd, John. *History of the Indian Archipelago.* Vol. 1. Edinburgh: Archibald Constable and Co., 1820.

Creese, Helen. *Women of the Kakawin World: Marriage and Sexuality in the Indic Courts of Java and Bali.* Armonk, N.Y.: M. E. Sharpe, 2004.

Cribb, Robert, ed. *The Late Colonial State in Indonesia: Political and Economic Foundations of the Netherlands Indies, 1880–1942.* Verhandelingen, no. 163, November 1994. Leiden: KITLV Press, 1994.

Davis, Natalie Zemon. *Fictions in the Archives: Pardon Tales and Their Tellers in Sixteenth-Century France.* Stanford, Calif.: Stanford University Press, 1987.

———. "Polarities, Hybridities: What Strategies for Displacement?" Unpublished paper.

———. *The Return of Martin Guerre.* Cambridge, Mass.: Harvard University Press, 1984.

———. *Women on the Margins: Three Seventeenth-Century Lives.* Cambridge, Mass.: Harvard University Press, 1995.

Diederiks, H. A. "Strafrecht en strafrechtspraktijk tijdens de Republiek in het bijzonder in de achttiende eeuw." *Holland Regionaal-Historisch Tijdschri—Strafrecht and Criminaliteit in de 18e Eeuw,* Achtste jaargang, no. 3 (June 1976): 99–107.

Dupin, A. M. J. J., and E. R. Lefebvre de Laboulaye. *Glossaire de l'ancien droit français.* Paris, 1846.

Elson, R. E. *The End of the Peasantry in Southeast Asia: A Social and Economic History of Peasant Livelihood, 1800–1990s.* New York: St. Martin's, 1997.

———. *Village Java under the Cultivation System, 1830–1870.* Sydney: Allen and Unwin, 1994.

Esterik, Penny van, ed. *Women of Southeast Asia.* Dekalb, Ill.: Northern Illinois University, Center for Southeast Asian Studies Monograph Series on Southeast Asia, Occasional Paper no. 17, 1982.

Eyck van Heslinga, E. S. van. *Van Compagnie naar Koopvaardij: De Scheepvaartverbinding van de Bataafse Republiek met de Kolonien in Azie, 1795–1806.* Amsterdam: De Bataafsche Leeuw, 1988.

Faber, Sjoerd. "Strafrechtspleging en criminaliteit te Amsterdam in de achtiende eeuw." *Holland Regionaal-Historisch Tijdschrift—Strafrecht and Criminaliteit in de 18e Eeuw,* Achtste jaargang, no. 3 (June 1976): 108–15.

Fasseur, Cornelis. *The Politics of Colonial Exploitation: Java, the Dutch, and the Cultivation System.* Ithaca, N.Y.: Cornell University, Southeast Asia Program, 1992.

Fernando, Radin. *Murder most Foul: A Panorama of Social Life in Melaka from the 1780s to the 1820s.* Kuala Lumpur: Malaysia, Mbras Mono, no. 38, 2006.

Foucault, Michel. *Discipline and Punish: The Birth of the Prison.* New York: Vintage, 1979.

Fox, James J., ed. *Indonesian Heritage: Religion and Ritual.* Singapore: Editions Didier Millet–Archipelago Press, 1999.

Furnivall, John S. *Colonial Policy and Practice: A Comparative Study of Burma and Netherlands India.* Cambridge: Cambridge University Press, 1948.

———. *Netherlands India: A Study of Plural Economy.* Cambridge: Cambridge University Press, 1939.

———. *Studies in the Social and Economic Development of the Netherlands East Indies: An Introduction to the History of the Netherlands India, 1602–1836.* Rangoon: University of Rangoon, Burma Book Club, 1934.

Gaastra, Femme S. *De Geschiedenis van de VOC.* Leiden: Walburg Press, 1991.

Geertz, Clifford. *Agricultural Involution: The Processes of Ecological Change in Indonesia.* Berkeley and Los Angeles: University of California Press, 1963.

———. *Negara: The Theatre State in Nineteenth-Century Bali.* Princeton, N.J.: Princeton University Press, 1980.

Ginzburg, Carlo. *The Cheese and the Worms: The Cosmos of a Sixteenth-Century Miller.* Baltimore: Johns Hopkins University Press, 1992.

———. *Clues, Myths, and the Historical Method.* Baltimore: Johns Hopkins University Press, 1992.

———. *The Night Battles: Witchcraft and Agrarian Cults in the Sixteenth and Seventeenth Centuries.* Baltimore: Johns Hopkins University Press, 1992.

Glamann, K. *Dutch-Asiatic Trade, 1620–1740.* 2nd ed. Den Haag: Martinus Nijhoff, 1981.

Gokkel, H. R. W., and N. van der Wal. *Juridisch Latijn.* 5de druk. Alphen aan den Rijn: Samsom H.D. Tjeenk Willink, 1991.

Goor, J. van. *De Nederlandse Koloniën: Geschiedenis van de Nederlandse expansie, 1600–1975.* Den Haag: Sdu Uitgeverij Koninginnegracht, 1994.

Gouda, Frances. *Dutch Culture Overseas: Colonial Practice in the Netherlands Indies, 1900–1942.* Amsterdam: Amsterdam University Press, 1995.

Grotius, Hugo. *The Jurisprudence of Holland.* Edited by R. W. Lee. Oxford: Clarendon Press, 1936.

Haan, F. C. de. *Oud Batavia.* Batavia: G. Kolff, 1922.

———. *Priangan: De Preanger-Regentschappen onder het Nederlandsch Bestuur tot 1811.* Batavia: G. Kolff, 1910.

———. *Uit Oude Notarispapeiren II, Andreas Cleyer.* Batavia: G. Kolff, 1903.

Hattum, M. van, and H. Rooseboom. *Glossarium van Oude Nederlandse Rechtstermen.* Amsterdam: Faculteit der Rechtsgeleerdheid, 1977.

Heckscher, Eli F. *Mercantilism.* London: George Allen, 1955.

Heijden, Manon van der. *Huwelijk in Holland: Stedelijke Rechtspraak en Kerkelijke Tucht, 1550–1700.* Amsterdam: Bert Bakker, 1998.

Hilferding, Rudolf. *Finance Capital: A Study of the Latest Phase of Capitalist Development.* London: Routledge, 1981.

Hoadley, Mason C. *An Introduction to Javanese Law: A Translation and Commentary on the Agama.* Tucson: Published for the Association for Asian Studies by the University of Arizona Press, 1981.

———. *Selective Judicial Competence: The Cirebon-Priangan Legal Administration, 1680–1792.* Ithaca, N.Y.: Cornell University, Southeast Asia Program Studies, 1994.

Hobsbawm, Eric J. *The Age of Empire, 1875–1914.* New York: Vintage, 1987.

Hobson, John Atkinson. *Imperialism: A Study.* Ann Arbor: University of Michigan Press, 1965.

Hodgart, Alan. *The Economics of European Imperialism.* New York: Norton, 1977.

Hogendorp, Dirk van. *Berigt van den Tegenwoordigen Toestand der Bataafsche Bezittingen in Oost-Indiën en den Handel op Dezelve; door Dirk van Hogendorp.* Delft: Published by the author, 1799.

Hoyt, Sarina Hayes. *Old Malacca.* Kuala Lumpur: Oxford University Press, 1996.

Huussen, A.H., Jr. "De rechtspraak in strafzaken voor het Hof van Holland in de eerste kwart van de achtiende eeuw." *Holland Regionaal-Historisch Tijdschrif—Strafrecht and Criminaliteit in de 18e Eeuw.* Achtste jaargang, no. 3 (June 1976): 116–39.

Huysers, Ary. *Beknopte Beschrijving der Oostindische Etablissementen.* Amsteldam: Roos, 1792; Cornell University, Echols Collection, Asia Rare.

Israel, Jonathan. *Dutch Primacy in World Trade, 1585–1740.* New York: Oxford University Press, 1989.

———. *The Dutch Republic: Its Rise, Greatness, and Fall, 1477–1806.* New York: Oxford, 1995.

Jacobs, Els M. *Koopman in Azië: De handel van de Verenigde Oost-Indische Compagnie tijdens de 18de eeuw.* Zutphen: Walburg Press, 2000.

Jacobsen, Trudy. "Apsara, Accoutrements, Activists: A History of Women and Power in Cambodia." Ph.D. dissertation, University of Queensland, 2004.

————. *Lost Goddesses: Female Power and Its Denial in Cambodian History.* Copenhagen: NIAS Press, 2006.

Jeske, Reijs, ed. *Vrouwen in de Nederlandse Kolonien.* Nijmegen: SUN, 1986.

Kartodirdjo, Sartono. *Indonesian Historiography.* Yogyakarta: Kanisius, 2001.

Kathirithamby-Wells, Jeyamalar. "Restraints on the Development of Merchant Capitalism in Southeast Asia before c. 1800." In Reid, *Southeast Asia in the Early Modern Era: Trade, Power, Belief,* 123–50.

Kelly, David, and Anthony Reid, eds. *Asian Freedoms: The Idea of Freedom in East and Southeast Asia.* Cambridge: Cambridge University Press, 1998.

Knaap, Gerritt J. *Kruidnagelen en Christenen: De Verenigde Oost-Indische Compagnie en de Bevolking van Ambon, 1656–1696.* Dordrecht: Foris, 1987.

————. "Pants, Skirts, and Pulpits: Women and Gender in Seventeenth-Century Amboina." In Andaya, *Other Pasts,* 147–73.

La Bree, J. *De Rechterlijke Organisatie en Rechtsbedeling te Batavia in de XVIIe Eeuw.* Rotterdam: Nijgh & Van Ditmar, 1951.

Ladurie, LeRoy Emmanuel. *Montaillou: Cathars and Catholics in a French Village, 1294–1324.* London: Scholar Press, 1978.

Lee, R. W. *An Introduction to Roman-Dutch Law.* London: Oxford University Press, 1925.

Leeuwen, Simon van. *Roomsch Hollandsch Recht.* London: Butterworth, 1820.

Legge, John. "The Writing of Southeast Asian History." Chapter 1 in *The Cambridge History of Southeast Asia: Volume One,* ed. Nicholas Tarling, 1–50. Cambridge: Cambridge University Press, 1992.

Lenin, Vladimir Ilich. *Imperialism: The Highest Stage of Capitalism.* New York: International Publishers, 1933.

Leur, Jacob Cornelius van. *Indonesian Trade and Society: Essays in Asian Social and Economic History.* The Hague: W. van Hoeve, 1967.

Lev, Daniel S. "Judicial Institutions and Legal Culture in Indonesia." In *Culture and Politics in Indonesia,* ed. Claire Holt, 246–318. Ithaca, N.Y.: Cornell University Press, 1972.

Linden, Johannes van der. *Institutes of Holland.* Translated by Henry Juta. Cape Town, 1884.

Locher-Scholten, Elsbeth. *Women and the Colonial State: Essays on Gender and Modernity in the Netherland Indies, 1900–1942.* Amsterdam: Amsterdam University Press, 2000.

Locher-Scholten, Elsbeth, and Anke Niehof, eds. *Indonesian Women in Focus: Past and Present Notions.* Dordrecht: Foris, 1987.

Luxemburg, Rosa. *The Accumulation of Capital.* New York: Monthly Review, 1951.

Marx, Karl, and Frederick Engels. *The Communist Manifesto.* Edited by Eric Hobsbawm. New York: Verso, 1998.

Meilink-Roelofsz, Marie Antoinette P. *Asian Trade and European Influence in the Indonesian Archipelago between 1500 and about 1630.* The Hague: Martinus Nijhoff, 1962.

———, ed. *De VOC in Azie*. Bussum: Fibula-Van Dischoeck, 1976.

Meilink-Roelofsz, M. A. P., R. Raben, and H. Spijkerman, eds. *The Archives of the Dutch East India Company, 1602–1795*. The Hague: ARA, 1992.

Mignolo, Walter D. *The Darker Side of the Renaissance: Literacy, Territoriality, Colonization*. Ann Arbor: University of Michigan Press, 1995.

Muir, Edward, and Guido Ruggiero, eds. *History from Crime*. Baltimore: Johns Hopkins University Press, 1994.

Müller, Brigitte. *Op de Wipstoel—De Niet-gewettigde Inheemse Vrouw van de Blanke Europeanen in Nederlands-Indie 1890–1940, een Literatuuronderzoek naar beeldvoorming en werkelijkheid*. Feministische Antropologie 10. Amsterdam: Vrije Universiteit, 1995.

Mus, Paul. *India Seen from the East: Indian and Indigenous Cults in Champa*. Clayton, Victoria: Monash University, Centre of Southeast Asian Studies, 1975.

Niemeijer, Hendrik E. *Batavia: een koloniale samenleving in de zeventiende eeuw*. Amsterdam: Balans, 2005.

———. *Calvinisme en koloniale stadscultuur Batavia, 1619–1725*. Almelo, Netherlands: Biester and Abbes, 1996.

———. "Slavery, Ethnicity, and the Economic Independence of Women in Seventeenth-Century Batavia." In Andaya, *Other Pasts*, 174–94.

Ollard, Richard. *Man of War: Sir Robert Holmes and the Restoration Navy*. London: Hodder and Stoughton, 1969.

Ong, Aihwa, and Michael G. Peletz, eds. *Bewitching Women, Pious Men: Gender and Body Politics in Southeast Asia*. Berkeley and Los Angeles: University of California Press, 1995.

Onghokam. "Inscrutable and the Paranoid: An Investigation into the Sources of the Brotodiningrat Affair." In *Southeast Asian Transitions: Approaches through Social History*, ed. Ruth T. McVey, 112–57. New Haven, Conn.: Yale University Press, 1978.

Orlers, J. J. *Beschrijvinge der Stadt Leyden*. Leiden, 1641.

Pombejra, Dhiravat na. "VOC Employees and Their Relationships with Mon and Siamese Women: A Case Study of Osoet Pegua." In Andaya, *Other Pasts*, 195–214.

Raben, Remco. "Batavia and Colombo: The Ethnic and Spatial Order of Two Colonial Cities, 1600–1800." Dissertation, Rijksuniversiteit Leiden, 1996.

Raffles, Sir Thomas Stamford. *Geschiedenis van Java*. Translated by J. E. de Sturler. Amsterdam: Gebroeders van Cleef, 1836.

———. *The History of Java*. 2 vols. London: John Murray, 1830.

Ramusack, Barbara N., and Sharon Sievers. *Women in Asia*. Bloomington: Indiana University Press, 1999.

Reid, Anthony. *Expansion and Crisis*. Volume 2 of *Southeast Asia in the Age of Commerce, 1450–1680*. New Haven, Conn.: Yale University Press, 1993.

———. "Female Roles in Pre-colonial Southeast Asia." *Modern Asian Studies* 22, no. 3 (1988): 629–45.

——, ed. *Indonesian Heritage: Early Modern History.* Singapore: Editions Didier Millet–Archipelago Press, 1996.

——. *The Lands below the Winds.* Volume 1 of *Southeast Asia in the Age of Commerce, 1450–1680.* New Haven, Conn.: Yale University Press, 1988.

——. "The Seventeenth-Century Crisis in Southeast Asia." *Modern Asian Studies* 24, no. 4 (1990): 639–59.

——, ed. *Slavery, Bondage, and Dependency in Southeast Asia.* New York: St. Martin's Press, 1983.

——, ed. *Southeast Asia in the Early Modern Era: Trade, Power, Belief.* Ithaca, N.Y.: Cornell University Press, 1993.

Ricklefs, Merle. *A History of Modern Indonesia since c. 1300.* Stanford: Stanford University Press, 2002.

Said, Edward. *Culture and Imperialism.* New York: Vintage, 1994.

——. *Orientalism.* New York: Vintage Books, 1994.

Schama, Simon. *The Embarrassment of Riches: An Interpretation of Dutch Culture in the Golden Age.* Berkeley and Los Angeles: University of California Press, 1988.

Schneider, Zoë A. "Women before the Bench: Female Litigants in Early Modern Normandy." *French Historical Studies* 23, no. 1 (Winter 2000): 1–32.

Scott, James C. *Domination and the Arts of Resistance: Hidden Transcripts.* New Haven, Conn.: Yale University Press, 1990.

——. *The Moral Economy of the Peasant: Rebellion and Subsistence in Southeast Asia.* New Haven, Conn.: Yale University Press, 1976.

——. *Weapons of the Weak: Everyday Forms of Peasant Resistance.* New Haven, Conn.: Yale University Press, 1985.

Scott, Joan. "Women's History." In *New Perspectives on Historical Writing,* ed. Peter Burke, 24–41. University Park: Pennsylvania State University Press, 1992.

Sears, Laurie J., ed. *Fantasizing the Feminine in Indonesia.* Durham: Duke University Press, 1996.

Sepp, D. *Repertorium op de Literatuur Betreffende de Nederlandsche Kolonien voor zoover zij verspreid is in tijdschriften, periodieken, serie- en mengelwerken.* Zevende vervolg 1926–1930 'S-Gravenhage: Martinus Nijhoff, 1935.

Smail, John R. W. "On the Possibility of an Autonomous History of South-East Asia." *Journal of Southeast Asian History* 2, no. 2 (July 1961): 73–105.

Smith, Woodruff D. *European Imperialism in the Nineteenth and Twentieth Centuries.* Chicago: Nelson-Hall, 1982.

Spence, Jonathan D. *The Death of Woman Wang.* New York: Viking Press, 1978.

——. *Treason by the Book.* New York: Viking Press, 2001.

Steensgaard, Niels. *The Asian Trade Revolution of the Seventeenth Century: The East India Companies and the Decline of the Caravan Trade.* Chicago: University of Chicago Press, 1974.

——. "The Seventeenth-Century Crisis and the Unity of Eurasian History." *Modern Asian Studies* 24, no. 4 (1990): 683–97.

Steinberg, David Joel, ed. *In Search of Southeast Asia: A Modern History.* Honolulu: University of Hawaii Press, 1985.

Stevens, Maila, ed. *Why Gender Matters in Southeast Asian Politics.* Clayton, Victoria: Monash University Southeast Asia Centre, Monash Papers on Southeast Asia no. 41, 1991.

Stoler, Ann Laura. *Carnal Knowledge and Imperial Power: Race and the Intimate in Colonial Rule.* Berkeley and Los Angeles: University of California Press, 2002.

———. *Race and the Education of Desire: Foucault's* History of Sexuality *and the Colonial Order of Things.* Durham: Duke University Press, 1995.

Tacitus. *The Agricola and Germania.* New York: Penguin, 1970.

Tamm, Ditlev. *Roman Law and European Legal History.* Copenhagen: DJØF Publishing, 1997.

Taylor, Jean Gelman. *Indonesia: Peoples and Histories.* New Haven: Yale University Press, 2003.

———. *The Social World of Batavia: European and Eurasian in Dutch Asia.* Madison: University of Wisconsin Press, 1983.

Toer, Pramoedya Ananta. *This Earth of Mankind.* New York: Penguin, 1996.

Tracy, James D., ed. *The Political Economy of Merchant Empires.* New York: Cambridge University Press, 1991.

———, ed. *The Rise of Merchant Empires: Long-Distance Trade in the Early Modern World, 1350–1750.* New York: Cambridge University Press, 1990.

Tran, Nhung Tuyet. "Vietnamese Women at the Crossroads: Gender and Society in Early Modern Dai Viet." Ph.D. dissertation, University of California, Los Angeles, 2004.

Valentijn, François. *Oud en nieuw Oost-Indien.* Dordrecht: J. van Braam, 1724–1726.

Valk, M. H. van der. "Nederlandsch Intestaat Erfrecht Buiten Europa." *Tijdschrift voor Rechtsgeschiedenis / Revue d'Histoire du Droit,* vol. 10, 412–464. Haarlem: Tjeenk Willink & Zoon, 1930.

Vollenhoven, C. van. *Staatsrecht Overzee.* Leiden: Stenfert Kroese, 1934.

Vries, Jan de. "Connecting Europe and Asia: A Quantitative Analysis of the Cape Route Trade, 1497–1795." Unpublished paper.

Vries, Jan de, and Ad van der Woude. *The First Modern Economy: Success, Failure, and Perseverance of the Dutch Economy, 1500–1815.* New York: Cambridge University Press, 1997.

Wessels, J. W. *History of the Roman-Dutch Law.* Grahamstown, Cape Colony: African Book Company, 1908.

Wie, Thee Kian. *Explorations in Indonesian Economic History.* Jakarta: Lembaga Penerbit, Fakultas Ekonomi, Universitas Indonesia, 1994.

Wiesner, Merry. *Women and Gender in Early Modern Europe.* Melbourne: Cambridge University Press, 1993.

Williams, Eric. *Capitalism and Slavery.* Chapel Hill: University of North Carolina Press, 1994.

Wolf, Eric R. *Europe and the People without History.* Berkeley and Los Angeles: University of California, 1982.

Wolters, Oliver W. *Early Indonesian Commerce: A Study of the Origins of Srivijaya.* Ithaca, N.Y.: Cornell University Press, 1967.

————. *The Fall of Srivijaya in Malay History.* Ithaca, N.Y.: Cornell University Press, 1970.

————. *History, Culture, and Region in Southeast Asian Perspectives.* Ithaca, N.Y.: SEAP, 1999.

Yeoh, Brenda S. A. *Power Relations and the Urban Built Environment in Colonial Singapore.* Kuala Lumpur: Oxford University Press, 1996.

Zainu'ddin, Alisa, ed. *Kartini Centenary: Indonesian Women, Then and Now.* Clayton, Victoria: Centre for Southeast Asian Studies, Monash University, 1980.

Zinoman, Peter. *Colonial Bastille: A History of Imprisonment in Vietnam, 1862–1940.* Berkeley and Los Angeles: University of California Press, 2001.

Index